Praise for *Black & White*

"Racial matters are always personal and always systemic. In this book, Hadra and Hambrick usher us through this tangle, ever mindful of the pivotal role of friendship. This is the route they have traveled together—the accessible but daunting road into the joy, pain, and hope of honest friendship. What first remakes their hearts, also resets their public lives. Read this book with a friend not like you, and let it do its powerful work!"

—*Mark Labberton*, President, Fuller Theological Seminary

"Are you tired feeling awkward, unequipped, defensive or afraid whenever social media chatter fires up about football and the national anthem, police shootings, or Black History Month? Teesha Hadra and John Hambrick synergize their backgrounds and perspectives to create a gospel-centered dialogue on race that will make you sweat at first. But, if you believe that the gospel can heal and transform, then grab this book and read it with a group of friends or your small group, God will use your courageous conversations to build bridges for the sake of gospel and heal what racism and segregation have devastated for 400 years. As an African American woman who spent 14 years as a leader at a predominantly white megachurch, I'm fist-pumping Teesha and John's courageous decision to blast the light of Christ on a difficult topic that far too many American churches (praise God, not mine!) are content to ignore."

—*Barb Roose*, speaker and author of *Winning the Worry Battle*

"Awareness creates discontent. A lack of awareness often results in complacency. When it comes to racism there's no room for complacency. Especially for Christ followers. In *Black & White* my friends Teesha Hadra and John Hambrick stir our awareness. My hope—their hope—is that having become aware we will become permanently and passionately discontent with racism in all of its insidious forms and expressions."

—*Andy Stanley*, pastor and founder of North Point Community Church, author of *Irresistible*

"Very few people want to talk about the pervasiveness of modern racism, but Teesha Hadra and John Hambrick make a compelling case for why we need to tackle the issue head-on, and they serve as a beautiful example of how to approach it. Their story is a refreshing reminder that when we start with relationships rooted in love and respect for one another, we can work through even the most uncomfortable and complex of challenges."

—***Bob Creson***, President/CEO, Wycliffe Bible Translators USA

TEESHA HADRA AND JOHN HAMBRICK

BLACK&

DISRUPTING RACISM ONE FRIENDSHIP AT A TIME

WHITE

ABINGDON PRESS
NASHVILLE

BLACK & WHITE
DISRUPTING RACISM ONE FRIENDSHIP AT A TIME

Copyright © 2019 by Abingdon Press

All rights reserved.

Library of Congress Cataloging-in-Publication Data has been requested.

ISBN 978-1-5018-7917-3

Excerpts from the Reverend Dr. Martin Luther King Jr. reprinted by arrangement with The Heirs to the Estate of Martin Luther King Jr., c/o Writers House as agent for the proprietor New York, NY.

Scripture quotations unless noted otherwise are from the Revised Standard Version of the Bible, copyright © 1946, 1952, and 1971 National Council of the Churches of Christ in the United States of America. Used by permission. All rights reserved worldwide. http://nrsvbibles.org/

Scripture quotations marked NASB are from the New American Standard Bible® (NASB), Copyright © 1960, 1962, 1963, 1968, 1971, 1972, 1973, 1975, 1977, 1995 by The Lockman Foundation. Used by permission. www.Lockman.org

Scripture quotations marked NIV are from the Holy Bible, New International Version®, NIV®. Copyright © 1973, 1978, 1984, 2011 by Biblica, Inc.™ Used by permission of Zondervan. All rights reserved worldwide. www.zondervan.com The "NIV" and "New International Version" are trademarks registered in the United States Patent and Trademark Office by Biblica, Inc.™

Scripture quotations marked NRSV are from the New Revised Standard Version Bible, copyright © 1989 National Council of the Churches of Christ in the United States of America. Used by permission. All rights reserved worldwide.

19 20 21 22 23 24 25 26 27—10 9 8 7 6 5 4 3 2 1

MANUFACTURED IN THE UNITED STATES OF AMERICA

To Mike Reimer and David Rohrer,
"friends along the way"

—J. D. H.

To Fred, my partner in all things,
"you have been God's grace to me."

—T. T. H.

CONTENTS

ACKNOWLEDGMENTS

We wish to thank the talented folks at Abingdon Press, including the wonderfully encouraging Susan Salley. She championed this book from the moment she heard about it. Her colleagues Tim Cobb, Elizabeth Pruitt, and Susan Cornell, along with many others, have also provided valuable assistance. Thanks to publicist Jason Jones of Jones Literary and his assistant publicist Sara Colley for helping us get the word out about *Black & White*. Lauren Winner, who edited the manuscript, is astoundingly good at what she does. Her perspective on our topic, command of the craft of writing, and insistence that we be clear and concise saved us time and again from what would have been embarrassing authorial blunders. Literary agent Blythe Daniel has shepherded us along through the whole process of getting this book written and published. When some told us, "No," she said, "Yes." When we said, "Maybe?" she said, "Certainly!" We are grateful beyond words.

I would like to thank Jasmine White, Phil Allen, Anastasia Fuentes, Esperanza Terrell, Caleb Campbell, and Mercy Young-McVay. Together, we have laughed, wept, prayed, and worked to bring about racial justice in our community. Thanks for being my teachers and my supporters. I want to thank my entire family, especially my mother, Jacinth, and my sister, Alicia. I was blessed to have been on

ACKNOWLEDGMENTS

the receiving end of their endless supply of love and encouragement. Finally, I want to thank the matriarch of my family, my grandmother, Ruth, who models the Christian life for me every day and on whose shoulders I stand. —Teesha

I would like to thank Terrence Smith, Nate and Traci Robinson, Sam Collier, Theron Nixon, Heath Ward, Leroy Lamar, Marquise and Krystal Cox, Ameera Joe, Lee Jenkins, Jason Cain, C. J. Stewart, and Candi Cylar. These friends patiently walked alongside me as I slowly figured out that "Houston, we have a problem." My son, John Jr., and my daughter, Carrell, never failed to cheer me on from the sidelines during the challenging process of getting this book written. And finally, thanks to my wife, Patty, who read everything I wrote before anyone else did. Her patience and honesty have shaped not only what I wrote but also who I am. —John

INTRODUCTION

This book was written by two friends. One is a young black woman who grew up in South Florida. Her family is from Jamaica. The other is an older white man. He grew up on the beach in Southern California. His family is from Ireland, England, and Germany. That's us! Teesha and John. By all accounts, ours is an unlikely friendship. But it's the unlikely nature of our friendship that laid the groundwork for this book.

That said, we didn't create a friendship so we could write a book. We'd been friends for years before the idea of this book even entered our minds. But this book is based on our experience—on what we've each learned, through our friendship, about racism, power, and honesty. The idea that racism can be disrupted by friendship is not an abstract concept for us. It's our reality.

We worked together for years in the same department on the staff of Buckhead Church, one of the campuses of North Point Ministries, in Atlanta, Georgia. Our daily interactions established trust and respect between us. The trust gave us the courage to be truthful with each other. When our conversations turned to racial issues, we were confident that the trust and respect that we'd built between us would hold up. It did.

Of course our friendship was not limited to church matters and racial issues. Genuine friendship is never limited to ideological discussions. It's much bigger than that. We laugh a lot. There is the occasional tear. Teesha met her husband in John's office. John officiated at their wedding two years later under a magnificent live oak tree in a vineyard in central California. And even in the midst of writing this book, we made time to talk about other things. The laughter continues. We realize we are writing about a very serious topic, but we don't take ourselves too seriously.

While this book focuses on the impact friendship can have in the battle against racism, we situate our consideration of friendship in a larger field: We talk about systemic racism. We talk, with sadness, about our country's racist history. We talk about the anger and fear that sometimes characterize conversation about race and diversity, especially when those conversations occur between people who don't look like each other. You'll notice that we present very few if any solutions to the complicated and often contentious issues we touch upon. Our aim is to get the problems out on the table for you to look at. We figure that if enough of us are looking at the problems together and asking good questions together, maybe solutions will start to emerge someday. We've included discussion questions at the end of each chapter—we hope these might promote reflection and conversation between you and a friend or within a small group.

We also hope that as you're reading, you'll sometimes feel inclined to cheer us on or shout "Amen!" We also suspect that you will occasionally become frustrated with us. You'll feel like we went too far or didn't go far enough. Sometimes, you'll think differently than we do about a particular topic. That's not a bad thing. If everybody thinks alike, nobody thinks very much.

So, thank you for picking up this book. Thank you for your patience with us. And most of all, thank you for caring enough to consider forming a friendship or two with someone who doesn't look like you. There's no better way to wade into the battle against racism than to wade into it together.

—John and Teesha

Chapter One

THE CLOCK IS TICKING

In this unfolding conundrum of life and history there is such a thing as being too late.

—Martin Luther King Jr.

Racism comes up a lot these days. It seems like it comes up—in conversation, on the news—much more than it did fifteen or twenty years ago. People who don't want to talk about racism find themselves frequently having to make a conscious choice to avoid the topic. But some people do want to talk about it.

John was in his office recently, catching up with a husband and wife who were friends of his. At some point, the topic of racism came up because of a job-related racial incident the husband had experienced. The tone of the conversation changed. John and his friends were no longer casually talking about restaurants and vacations and families. They were talking about something that had caused the couple a great deal of angst. You could feel the pain in the room. You could see it in everyone's eyes, in their body language. John and his friends were grieved by the presence of a great evil that shouldn't exist in this country but does. What could be done to wipe this ugly stain away?

A few days later, John found himself in another conversation about racism. The news that morning had carried the story of an unarmed black man who had been shot and killed by a white police officer. After exchanging some pleasantries with his friend, John's conversation took the following turn:

"Hey, did you hear about that shooting up in Chicago?" asked John.[1]

"Yeah, I did. It's too bad." The tone of John's friend was flat—no anger, no angst, no pain.

"It's crazy how this keeps happening."

"That's true," said John's friend, "but when you think about the thousands of interactions that happen every day between the police and people, some bad stuff is bound to happen occasionally."

Clearly John's friend was talking about something that had little to do with his world—or he couldn't perceive the connections between their discussion of racism and his life. The conversation moved on to other things.

Then it happened again. Racism came up while John was talking to yet another friend. Without missing a beat, this guy immediately began to critique the black community. He focused on what he believed were sweeping and serious moral failures. It was clear that he thought we couldn't talk about racism until the black community got its act together. Or so he said.

One topic. Three friends. Three distinct responses.

As we reflected on this, we were reminded that everyone is entitled to his or her opinion; but it's appropriate to consider whether an opinion is consistent with reality: Is racism endemic in contemporary America or not? Is it a big deal or not? Is it getting better or getting worse? How does it operate? Who's responsible for fixing it?

To answer those important questions, we decided to use Google to take a "snapshot" of the state of racial relations in our country. We selected October 19, 2017, just a day before we wrote the sentence you're reading right now. We didn't want to know what happened in 1868, or 1954, or 1973. We wanted to know what was going on this week. Here's what we found:

Pittsburgh, PA	A black woman is beaten with a brick by some white people who are angry over a racial incident that occurred at a public elementary school.
Gainesville, FL	A white supremacist rally is held at the University of Florida.
Atmore, AL	Another black man is executed by the state of Alabama.
Boston, MA	A student rally is held to protest a pair of on-campus racist incidents.
Houston, TX	A white couple, driving a pickup truck, pull up beside a black woman at an intersection. After hurling racist insults at her, they follow her into a neighborhood and ram her car with their truck, after which they immediately leave the scene.

These incidents literally happened yesterday (or, by the time you're reading this, a year ago, or fourteen months ago, or eighteen months ago). They happened in the South and they happened in the North. They may have happened in your hometown. They're not the way things were. They're the way things are.

We should point out that there's nothing special about October 19. Go ahead and pick another date. It could be February 18 or July 21 or December 5. Do a Google search on the day you select. Type in "racist incidents" and enter the date you picked along with the current year. You'll likely find a comparable number of stories.

We can (and should) think about these stories as *stories that involved members of our human family*. They contain incidents where fellow family members were abused. If you are an American, we hope you are thinking about these stories *as an American*. The people who were denigrated and injured stood in line beside us when we voted. They wept with us when 9/11 happened. And some would die, serving alongside us in the armed forces.

But most importantly, we hope that if you identify as a Christian, you are thinking as these stories *as a Christian*. The evil acts they contain were committed against someone created in God's image. The pain was inflicted upon those for whom Jesus Christ died. In light of this, nobody should be more disturbed about these stories than we Christians.

> *If you are an American, we hope you are thinking about these stories* **as an American. The people who were denigrated and injured stood in line beside us when we voted. They wept with us when 9/11 happened. And some would die, serving alongside us in the armed forces.**

The idea that Christians should be profoundly disturbed by all this is not a new idea. It was not cooked up by a cell of over-the-top Christian radicals meeting somewhere in a back room. This idea is firmly rooted in the texts of the Old and New Testaments. It reflects the compassion that has always represented the best and healthiest expressions of the Christian faith: it is normal and appropriate and essential for Christians to be upset by these stories of racial violence. But the time has come for Christians to consider something more.

People who call Jesus their Lord and Savior can no longer afford to merely engage in idle, albeit distressed, conversation about racism. At best, the watching world reads our inaction as proof of our irrelevance. At worst, we give the world another reason to reject the gospel. The church cannot let that stand. It's not too late to turn things around, but the clock is ticking. The time to act to combat racism is now.

We've met plenty of Christians—that is, plenty of white Christians—who have a tendency to look the other way when it comes to racism. When pressed, they say that things have gotten better and that if we stir things up, we might make things worse. Well, clearly things are already pretty stirred up, and ignoring evil in the hope that it will go away has never worked. Ignoring evil just makes it easier for evil to spread.

Other white Christians, upon hearing stories about black women being verbally insulted and then rammed with a truck, are flat-out surprised. Of course, they know about the big stories that everyone hears about in the news. But they thought those were isolated events. They are shocked to discover that the tip of the iceberg actually has a huge iceberg underneath.

Black people, on the other hand, are neither shocked nor surprised. They know about these stories because they keep happening. They keep happening to them, to their friends, and to their family members.

We recently hosted a small round-table conversation in Atlanta, Georgia. The topic was race and racism. We invited ten black people and five white people. We started things off by asking everybody to talk about how racism has affected their lives. Every black person in the room had a story to tell. Some talked about being personally insulted. Others were not considered for a promotion within their company. One guy talked about being pulled over by a police officer for what's come to be called the "crime" of driving while black, or DWB. He wasn't speeding. His taillights and brake lights were in perfect working order. His car registration was current. He wasn't drunk. He was staying in his lane. He was stopped because he was black. This became obvious when the officer referred to our friend as "boy" and demanded he get out of the car. When the driver didn't move fast enough to suit the officer, he was slammed face-down on the ground and asked what he thought he was doing driving around "here" at night.

The most painful story we heard had to do with a lady who attended a social event at a local, predominantly white church. She had just started worshipping there and was looking forward to getting to know some of the people with whom she worshipped on Sunday morning. This church is made up of middle-class people. They are well educated. They tend to have professional jobs. They dress well and are fairly sophisticated. And all those things described this lady. She fit right in. She looked forward to becoming a part of this community. As it was a family event, she brought along her five-year-old daughter. She was eager for both of them to get to know some of the other people in the church.

It's true that she and her daughter stood out because they were new and because they were the only black people there that day. But this church had a reputation for being a welcoming congregation, eager to make newcomers feel at home. Yet nobody talked to them for pretty much the whole event. Her daughter wondered what was wrong. Imagine having to explain all this to a little five-year-old who doesn't know that being black is a reason to be excluded.

At our meeting, all the black people had stories like this to tell. The white people had nothing comparable to share. They just sat and listened. It was awkward. They wanted to say something to make the tension go away. They wanted to link arms, pray, and sing "Kum Ba Yah," as we all walked out into a brand-new world where the sun was shining and the birds were singing and everybody loved each other. Instead, we settled for creating a safe place where peoples' stories could be heard. Our black friends kindly said it was a good start, but it was painfully obvious that, in the land of the free and the home of the brave, not everyone is equally free and not everyone is brave enough to do something about it. But some people are.

Let's turn the clock back again. This time let's turn it back a little further, back to 1971. A white sixth-grade kid in Houston, Texas, decides to invite a black sixth-grade kid over to his house for dinner. No big deal, right? It didn't get on the evening news. It didn't generate any publicity. But it made a difference. It turns out that the black kid who got invited to the white kid's house was named David Brown. Fast-forward thirty-nine years. David Brown is the chief of police in Dallas, Texas. On his watch, a racially motivated sniper shot fourteen Dallas police officers. Five of those officers died. It was July 7, 2016.

When the news conference regarding the shootings was held, an entire nation leaned in to listen as Brown tried to make sense of things. During his comments, he talked about that dinner with a white family to which he was invited so long ago. He said,

> I felt like Sidney Poitier in *Guess Who's Coming to Din-*
> *ner*. It really was one of those surreal moments when
> you don't know whether you're going to be uninvited.
> And his mother comes out with pot pies, and we sit

there and have a really nice dinner, and they made me feel at home. And they made me feel no different than them.[2]

Brown says he carries that memory with him when confronting racism. Brown further reflects,

I wonder why aren't we smarter than 6th graders? Why can't we figure this out? It takes not a big group, not yelling and screaming, but let's sit down and listen to each other and invite someone home for dinner.[3]

So, it turns out that a little white kid back in 1971 did something that, forty-four years later, would help a nation as it continued to struggle with racism. The dinner invitation didn't stop the shootings, but it set an example that modeled the importance of relationships in addressing issues of race. And it gave David Brown a place to stand as he confronted the chaos of racist hatred.

Then there's Daryl Davis, a black man who currently spends his time by trying to befriend members of the Ku Klux Klan. He's met dozens of Klansmen over the years. Some of them are open to Daryl's efforts. Some are not. Once in a while he encounters a violent reaction. But it's not unusual for the Klansmen, once they get over the shock of encountering a friendly black man, to engage in a conversation. Davis often begins by asking a simple question: "How can you hate me when you don't even know me?"[4] As a result, over the years he's seen a significant number of men leave the Klan. One eventually asked him to be his daughter's godfather. And yes, Daryl Davis is a Christian.

Both of these stories demonstrate a relational approach to disrupting racism, which is what this book is about. Through our friendship we have developed a deep and abiding trust in one another. That trust has freed us, and our spouses, to ask each other some hard questions, questions that black and white people desperately need to ask one another. And it's given us the confidence to know that the answers, when there are answers, will be given from a place of kindness and respect, even when those answers are hard to hear.

Each and every one of us can pursue friendships across "the color line." And it's these friendships that have the enormous potential to disrupt racism. A few of us might make some speeches, but millions of us have the opportunity to go speak with the people next door. A few of us might engage in a peaceful march down Main Street, but millions of us can march across the street and invite our neighbor over for dinner.

To make a friend, you don't have to be an expert on anything. You don't have to be up on all the current events. You can be young or old, black or white, Hispanic or Asian, rich or poor. You can listen to hip-hop or country, jazz or metal. You can have a PhD or be a high school dropout. None of that matters. What does matter is this: God—the God who calls us friend—wants to use you and your capacity for friendship to derail racism.

> *When all is said and done, disrupting racism is a Jesus thing.*

So, that's the offer on the table. It's not a new offer. God has always asked His people to fight against injustice and prejudice. That fight is not a liberal thing or a conservative thing. Neither is it a Democrat thing nor a Republican thing nor a Libertarian thing. It's not a mega-church thing or a mainline denominational thing. It's not a white thing or a black thing or an Asian thing or a Latin thing. When all is said and done, disrupting racism is a Jesus thing.

Since following Jesus is always an adventure, it's time to fasten your seatbelts. What follows is a collection of stories, information, perspectives, and practical, actionable ideas that will enable you to participate in what God is doing to disrupt racism. But be advised: whenever God is at work, there is always opposition. And all too often that opposition comes from where you least expect it—from folks who are in church on Sunday morning. But God's not worried. He has your back. All we have to do is accept Jesus's invitation to "Follow me." When we follow Him, we'll see Him change things. And we'll see Him do it through us, one relationship at a time.

DISCUSSION QUESTIONS

1. When you think about the Christians you know, do you think racism is a "front-burner" issue for them or a "back-burner" issue? Is it a front-burner or a back-burner issue for you? Do you think you've given enough attention to this issue? Why or why not?

2. Have you ever experienced or observed a racially charged incident? What happened?

3. Are your views on racism, racial reconciliation, and racial justice pretty much set or are they changing? Why? If they're changing, how are they changing? If they're set, when did they become set?

4. Is the idea of having a friend who doesn't look like you a potentially new experience or something you've been doing for a while? If it's a new idea, how are you feeling about it? If it's something you've experienced already, how did the friendship get started?

Chapter Two

IT'S PERSONAL

People are trapped in history and history is trapped in them.

—James Baldwin

I (Teesha) am a black person living in America. My blackness is with me when I wake up each morning, when I go to bed at night, and at every moment in between. Being a black person in America affects how I experience virtually every aspect of life. I suspect that most people who identify as a person of color would say the same, though each of us has our own story to tell about how the state of race relations in this country has shaped our lives. This is my story about how my blackness manifested as a feeling of "otherness" as I floated between two worlds that never seemed to come together.

One of my earliest memories of otherness occurred in elementary school. My parents sent my sister and me to a local Catholic school, although that was not our faith tradition. We rarely attended church, and when we did, we went to a Baptist church. The school was predominantly white; I was one of three black students in my grade. As part of the curriculum, the entire school gathered to attend Mass each week. My class would exit the classroom and form a line before walking to Mass. Because I was not Catholic, I had to take my place in the back of the line. I remember noticing that the two or three other black students in my class were in the back of the line with me. We were in the back of the line because of our religious affiliation. Our race was merely incidental. But as a young child, I didn't have the perspective to make that distinction. I just felt different.

Both of my parents were born in Jamaica and immigrated to the United States as young adults. By the time I came along in the early 1980s, my parents had settled in South Florida. My race and status as a child of working-class immigrant parents were not at all odd for South Florida. But even in a diverse context like South Florida, I could not escape the reality of racism in America. Even as my parents sent my sister and me to a predominantly white Catholic school during our formative years, they were intentional about instilling in us a pride about the color of our skin. My parents enrolled us in a program through the local chapter of the Urban League, where we were surrounded by other high-achieving black students and adults. Through this program we learned the soaring and pride-inducing lyrics of "Lift Every Voice and Sing," the song written by James Weldon Johnson, known in my community as the Black National Anthem. We also traveled to the annual matchup between the football teams of Florida A&M University and Bethune-Cookman College, both historically black universities in Florida. One Hawaiian Barbie was the extent of diversity in our doll collection, which was made up mostly of black dolls. It was important to our parents that we saw ourselves as beautiful, our skin as beautiful, and our hair as beautiful. My parents were attempting to combat a social norm in which white standards of beauty are dominant, where "nude" lipstick is clearly not referring to me, where even Band-Aids are not made with me in mind.

My family lived in a solidly working-class neighborhood. Our house was an unassuming three-bedroom, two-bath home with a large front and back yard, complete with multiple fruit trees. The only white people I can recall ever living in our neighborhood lived next door. They were very friendly people, though I cannot say our families were friends. They moved when I was in middle school, which seemed, at least in my mind, to solidify the status of the neighborhood as being nearly 100 percent black. My mother just sold the house I grew up in a couple of years ago; the neighborhood had remained a predominantly black neighborhood even decades after we first moved in and still is to this day.

I nonetheless encountered a wide array of races and cultures at every phase of my upbringing. If you are from or have visited South Florida, even if only to pass through on your way to catch a cruise ship, you know that South Florida is an exceptionally diverse part of the country. Imagine the laid-back ethos of Californian culture, pumped up with Latin and Caribbean flavors, and a Northeastern edginess, thanks to the many transplants from New York. That is home for me: diverse and vibrant—though also marked by racism and prejudice.

As a teenager, I knew that I should not open my purse or any other bag while in a store. To do so would put me at risk for being accused of stealing. I can't say for sure whether this was a specific lesson that my parents taught me or if it was an instinctive response to my own experience of otherness. Either way, I went through adolescence with an undeniable sense that others would make snap judgments about me because of my race.

Race continued to be a factor during my high school years. My mother didn't think the school I was zoned for would be up to snuff. I was accepted to a "magnet" high school and was bussed across town to another public high school. At the time, I never thought about the tax system that underwrote my mother's judgments about which school was suitable for me. I did not yet understand the extent to which public schools are funded by property taxes, which often leaves schools in predominantly minority neighborhoods underfunded and under-resourced in comparison to their suburban, majority-white counterparts.

While in high school, I was active on the debate team. When I say "active," I mean very active. My three best friends were also on the debate team, and we spent summers at debate camp. I will make no effort to conceal my nerdiness here. My debate team was actually very diverse, which I am sure was due in no small part to the magnet program. However, when we traveled to competitions, our team was clearly the outlier. By and large, the other teams were predominantly white. I was a black girl participating in what appeared to be a decidedly "white" activity. The sense of otherness was inescapable. Simultaneously, I had one of my earliest experiences with the "tyranny of low expectations." I can recall more than one occasion when I received the pseudo-compliment, "Oh, you speak so well," which was typically accompanied by what seemed like the slightest tinge of surprise. I was taught to respect adults, so I would smile and politely say, "Thank you." However, inside I was giving them major side-eye. I did not see my white counterparts receiving these same "compliments." My sense was that, because of my race, I was not even expected to have a basic command of the English language. I cannot comment with any certainty about my interlocutors' intent—probably, they were not harboring overtly racist thoughts. Probably, they were well-meaning people who thought they were saying something nice.

But I can tell you how I experienced their comments: I knew the white debaters were paid different compliments than I was paid. I knew debate judges and coaches looked at me and set low expectations of my performance. When I exceeded their low expectations, it was worthy of comment.

After high school, I attended the University of Florida, a predominantly white institution. As a textbook extrovert, I had no shortage of friends. But my friendships were segregated: I had a group of white friends and a group of black friends, but the two rarely, if ever, came together. In college, I joined a historically black sorority, Delta Sigma Theta. The organization was founded at Howard University in 1913, a time when

I knew debate judges and coaches looked at me and set low expectations of my performance. When I exceeded their low expectations, it was worthy of comment.

most institutions of higher education were closed to people who looked like me. The "white" fraternities and sororities had their parties on the weekend, as did the "black" fraternities and sororities. With perhaps a few exceptions, black people went to the "black" parties and white people went to the "white" parties. Your race determined how you spent your weekend, and at least at my university, there were not frequent occasions for the races to mix socially. I recall one weekend when a "black" fraternity and a "white" fraternity had a joint party at the latter's fraternity house. It was an anomaly, black people and white people on the campus of the University of Florida partying together, laughing together, telling stories together, and simply being with one another. Why did we choose to spend nearly all of our time in silos when life outside our silos, life together, seemed so rich?

After I graduated from college, I remained at the University of Florida for law school. When I finished law school, I began a career as a young attorney trying to navigate law-firm life. As I was settling into a niche practice area within insurance defense, I was hired as an associate attorney at an Atlanta law firm that had about a hundred lawyers, which made it a medium-sized firm. When I started, there were only two other black associates and one black partner. Another black female attorney started a few weeks after I did. There were no black male attorneys. Over time, increasing attention was paid to diversifying the firm's employees, and the face of the firm changed. Nonetheless, my work at this firm—indeed, all my work as an attorney—was like being on the high school debate team all over again: a black woman engaged in a white man's activity. Again, the sense of "otherness" was pervasive.

> *Why did we choose to spend nearly all of our time in silos when life outside of our silos, life together, seemed so rich?*

I did find a committed advocate in that firm: a middle-aged white male partner. He challenged, trusted, and empowered me. This partner actively helped me build my own client base, which is essential for an associate to "make partner," the pinnacle of law-firm life. This experience showed me the personal and professional impact of having an ally, and it showed me that support may come from the most unexpected places.

I'd been practicing law successfully for nearly seven years when God interrupted and called me to full-time ministry at Buckhead Church in Atlanta. Little did I know that issues of race would come to the forefront of my work there. Nor did I anticipate encountering yet another unexpected ally when I met John Hambrick, also a middle-aged white man. You will read more about my friendship with John and the impact that friendship has had on both of us in other parts of the book.

As I reflect on my experience of race over the course of my life, I am acutely aware of God's grace, for I know that it is only by this grace that my story is not one of having violent encounters with the police, heated confrontations with strangers, or racial slurs directed toward me. However, far too many people of color in America can recount such events as part of their stories. This is the source of much heartbreak for me, and like Martin Luther King Jr. in his famous "I Have a Dream" speech, my prayer is that justice would "roll down like waters, and righteousness like an ever-flowing stream" (Amos 5:24). That justice has a long way to roll is one of the reasons we decided to write this book.

DISCUSSION QUESTIONS

1. In her story, Teesha describes a "feeling of otherness." What did she mean by that? Have you ever felt that way? What contributed to that feeling?

2. During Teesha's tenure on her high school debate team, she experienced what she refers to as the "tyranny of low expectations." In other words, some white people were surprised that, as a black person, she was well-spoken. Do you think this is a common bias among white people? Why or why not? Do you think this phenomenon is becoming more or less common? On what do you base your answer? Do you think black people are sometimes tempted to think about white people in a certain way that is not necessarily justified?

3. How did you think a black woman's experience of racism might differ from that of a black man's?

4. Teesha talks about two advocates or allies she encountered, one in her law firm and one at Buckhead Church. What has been your experience of receiving the advocacy of another or being an advocate yourself? What sort of a difference did it make in your life? Why is this kind of relationship particularly important when it crosses racial boundaries? Have you ever seen a black person advocate for a white person?

Chapter Three

I ONCE WAS BLIND BUT NOW
I'M JUST KINDA NEARSIGHTED

Everyone is looking, not many are seeing.

—*Peter M. Leschak*

When I (John) was a little boy, the only black people I saw were on TV playing baseball. Bob Gibson. Maury Wills. Hank Aaron. Willie Mays. Willie McCovey. Jim Gilliam. Ernie Banks. John Roseboro. Fifty years later, their names flow effortlessly onto the page. The fact that they were black was of no more interest to me than their shoe size. All that mattered was that they were shining stars in my little-boy baseball universe. They existed alongside Sandy Koufax, who was Jewish; Juan Marichal, who was Dominican; and Whitey Ford, an aptly named white guy who pitched for the New York Yankees.

It never registered in my young mind that while these black

athletes were being cheered on the field, off the field it was a different story. Thousands of white people celebrated when Willie Mays hit a home run or when Bob Gibson pitched a shutout.[1] But once the game was over, many of those same white baseball fans would insist that people who looked like Willie Mays or Bob Gibson should sit in the back of the bus or drink from a different water fountain. They didn't mind watching the likes of Hank Aaron or Ernie Banks play ball, but they didn't want their kids going to school together. This went unnoticed by me. My Aaron and Mays baseball cards were sandwiched between the cards of their white counterparts. It was a fully integrated pack. I never thought about the fact that in real life such things were often not allowed.

It's not that there weren't plenty of opportunities for me to realize something was wrong. Many of the events that defined the civil rights movement occurred during the first twelve years of my life. I was in Southern California, taking my first steps in 1955, the year Emmett Till was murdered in Mississippi. That same year, in Montgomery, Alabama, Rosa Parks refused to sit in the back of the bus. In 1960 a group of brave students integrated the Woolworth's diner in Greensboro, North Carolina. That was about the same time I went to see my first Dodger game. The Freedom Riders' bus was firebombed just outside of Anniston, Alabama, on Mother's Day in 1961. On that same day, I gave my mom a Mother's Day card I'd drawn for her under the watchful eye of my second-grade teacher, Mr. Jack Pardee, at Calvert Street Elementary School in the San Fernando Valley.

> *It never registered in my young mind that while these black athletes were being cheered on the field, off the field it was a different story.*

On Wednesday, August 28, 1963, Dr. Martin Luther King Jr. gave his iconic "I Have a Dream" speech on the Mall in Washington, DC. I was nine. I have no memory of seeing that event on the evening news—I'm pretty sure I didn't even know it happened until several years later when we were studying civil rights in my eighth-grade social studies class. Later in 1963, on Sunday, September 15, to be exact, Thomas Edwin Blanton Jr. and three fellow members of the Ku Klux Klan set off sixteen sticks of dynamite underneath the 16th Street Baptist Church in Birmingham, Alabama. Four black schoolgirls, all just a little older than I, were killed by the blast. They had been in the church basement, putting on their choir robes to sing in the morning worship service. It was years before that got on my radar and even longer before it broke my heart.

It would have been unusual for a little white boy to spend much time thinking about these things. But it's nonetheless revealing that these events went virtually unnoticed by me until years later. I remember exactly where I was when John F. Kennedy was shot. I remember all the impassioned things the adults in my world said about his death. But I have only the faintest of memories about the civil rights movement, and I can't recall any adults in my life who seemed to care much about the suffering and injustice woven into that struggle.

As I reflected on this as an adult, I realized the three institutions that are supposed to contribute to the moral education of a little boy rang silent for me as black people suffered for the cause of racial justice. I don't recall hearing much about Jim Crow or violence toward black Americans at my elementary school. The subject never came up at the church we attended. And while my family talked about all sorts of things around the dinner table, we never talked about racial inequality.

It's not that my family was unusual in this regard. The problem was we were normal. And normal didn't mean that we were racist. Normal meant that we were isolated. We were a white, middle-class family surrounded by white middle-class families. The civil rights movement didn't appear to have anything to do with us. It didn't seem to affect our neighborhood or our church. It didn't make a difference at my school. All my dad's colleagues were white. All my mom's friends were white. It was as if the civil rights movement was happening on another planet. And in the meantime, our planet maintained its own orbit, light years away from Montgomery and Birmingham. My church, my elementary school, and my family didn't teach me to think bad things about black people. They taught me to not think about black people at all.

This began to change when I entered adolescence. The middle school I attended in Ventura, California, started to weave the events of the civil rights movement into our social studies classes. My teachers (still all white) asked us to think about things we'd never been asked to think about before. Yet it was all academic to me. I became aware of the events and their cultural significance, but my heart was uninvolved. Dr. King's assassination was merely a current event, unfortunate but irrelevant to my white adolescent world. I was told that I should care about these things. But I didn't, not in any real way—not until 1974, when I bumped into a guy named Bobby.

> *My church, my elementary school, and my family didn't teach me to think bad things about black people. They taught me to not think about black people at all.*

I met him during my sophomore year at Pepperdine University. It was at a meeting of InterVarsity Christian Fellowship. It was Bobby's first time there, and he stood out. He was a member of Pepperdine's nationally ranked men's volleyball team. He was a full-blown extrovert who lit up the meeting with positive energy. And he was black, the only black person in the room.

After the meeting concluded, I introduced myself. I was one of the student leaders of the group and wanted to make sure new people felt welcome. As Bobby and I talked, we discovered that we both surfed. Pepperdine, by the way, is right across the street from the Pacific Ocean. You can see the waves at Malibu Beach from the cafeteria. It wasn't too long after we met that we started surfing together, and thus began a friendship that began to change my life.

I suspect there's an app now that can be used to find surfable waves. But back in the day, the only way to find 'em was to hop in the car and drive up and down the coast. There are several places within a half hour of Pepperdine that are famous surf spots: Malibu, Leo Carrillo State Beach, County Line, Point Dume. But the thing is the waves aren't always breaking at all those spots, so you have to drive around to see what's happening. As a result, Bobby and I spent a lot of hours in the car talking as we hunted for waves. I got to know Bobby pretty well. He had a contagious sense of humor. He was five feet nine inches tall and had a vertical jump of over forty inches. That's why he made Pepperdine's volleyball team.

I learned some other things about Bobby as well. I learned about what it was like for a black man to attend a predominantly white university. I learned that black people and white people have a different take on the state of race relations in the United States. And I got a unique insight into what it was like for a black man to participate in what was almost exclusively a white man's sport.

Once we found some surfable waves, we would park, suit up, and walk into the water until it got deep enough to paddle out. Because there are a lot of surfers in Southern California, the places we went were always pretty crowded. In the two years we surfed together, Bobby was always the only black guy in the water. Always. Guys would give him the side-eye glance. They weren't hostile. They were just curious. When I caught a wave, nobody cared. I was just another white, blond surfer dude. But when Bobby caught a wave, everybody was watching to see if this black guy knew what he was doing. As a result, Bobby always felt like he was on display. He pointed out that it's hard to enjoy yourself when you're being stared at like some sort of carnival sideshow. And this was Bobby's life—a black man in a white man's world, in the water and on campus.

Had this been a story I'd read about in a novel, I doubt I would have cared very much. After all, I was not aware of any sensational examples of hate-filled bigotry at Pepperdine. No exclusions. No insults to speak of. But it was the first time I realized that someone I cared about had no choice but to struggle with—and against—racism. A struggle with race was happening to somebody I cared about. It was the first time I saw things from a black man's point of view—and gradually, I began to understand that outside of Pepperdine, things happened to Bobby that made surfing with white guys seem like a walk in the park. And for the first time, it bothered me. But it was no longer just about an individual. Because I cared about Bobby, I began to care about the struggles virtually all black people routinely endured.

I wish I could tell you that as a result of my friendship with Bobby, I soon became actively involved in the work of racial reconciliation. But things for me moved at a slow, uneven pace. After Pepperdine, I went to Fuller Theological Seminary. There I began to put some theological muscle around the bare bones of my growing concern about racism. William Pannell, a black professor, and Paul Jewett, a white professor, both made significant contributions to my thinking. They taught me that the first thing to embrace about any human being, white or black, Asian, Indian, or Hispanic, was that they were created in the image of God. As such, we all deserved to be treated with respect and dignity. They taught me that there was no such thing as a "social gospel" or a "personal gospel." There was only one gospel, and it was concerned about the totality of human existence, not only in the next life but in the one we're living right now. As a result, I graduated from Fuller with the conviction that working toward racial reconciliation was not a distraction from the work of preaching the gospel but was actually a part of that work.

I took that perspective to my first job as a pastor to high school students at Community Presbyterian Church, an all-white congregation in my hometown of Ventura, California. It lay dormant there for a while, but things changed again when I met John Perkins.

John Perkins is hard to pin down. He's an evangelist, but he's also a community developer. He's a civil rights activist, but he's also an educator. He's an author who speaks all over the world. He is a progressive who lobbies for values that are rooted in ancient traditions. In 1984, I spent the better part of a week with Dr. Perkins, and he left me different than he found me.

John tells his story in the book *Let Justice Roll Down*.[2] Born in 1930 in New Hebron, Mississippi, John lived the first seventeen years of his life in extreme poverty, tragedy, hopelessness, and the crushing bigotry that characterized the lives of black sharecroppers in the South. When his brother Clyde was killed by a white police officer, John was convinced that if he stayed in Mississippi, he would die a similar death. So, in 1947, he moved to a suburb of Los Angeles.

While in Southern California, John married and started a family. In 1957, he became a Christian. God led him to move to Mendenhall, Mississippi, where he began Voice of Calvary Ministries. The next twenty-two years saw John engaged in an incredible breadth of activity. He was involved in everything from teaching Sunday school to holding evangelistic rallies. He helped desegregate an all-white public high school. He started health clinics. He opened thrift stores and created housing cooperatives. This was all done in service to Jesus Christ, whom John came to realize cared deeply about the suffering of the black community—in Mississippi and everywhere else.

John's work drew international acclaim and attention. It also called down the wrath of the white people in the community who were committed to protecting and preserving the "southern way of life." John suffered at their hands.

By the time I met Dr. Perkins, he had moved back to Southern California. This time it wasn't to escape but rather to spread the work he had started in Mississippi. He realized that the racial evils that plagued the South were also wreaking havoc in California. He bought a house in northwest Pasadena, which, at the time, had the highest daytime crime rate in the country. Out of his home, he and his family launched the Harambee Christian Family Center.

I had contacted him through his publisher, where my wife worked as a graphic designer. We arranged to bring down a group of ten high school students during spring break. The Perkinses had been in their home for only a few months and needed some help getting things in shape. Our job would consist of cleaning out the vacant lot behind their home; it had become a sort of dump. We would do the cleanup necessary to turn it into a mini park/playground.

We stayed with the Perkinses for about four days. It was a little like being on the front line of a battlefield. The neighborhood looked rough and run down. The week before we arrived, someone had thrown a Molotov cocktail through the Perkinses' living room window. John considered it a sort of "welcome to the neighborhood."

The house next door to John's place was called a "drug house." It sold a variety of drugs to a variety of people. They would drive up at all hours of the day and night as if they were dropping by the local 7-Eleven to pick up a bag of Doritos. Over the course of the four days, we occasionally saw the men who ran that operation. Making eye contact with them felt risky. Their backyard contained three or four pit bulls chained to stakes in the ground.

Everybody in that neighborhood was black. The white skin of our little "mission team" made us stand out. People in the neighborhood openly stared at us. The police who patrolled the neighborhood asked us what on earth we were doing there. John Perkins just smiled.

That experience was God's next step for me in wrestling with racism. I left with more questions than answers. Why were all the people in John's neighborhood black? And why was the team we brought from Ventura all white? Why were there no Molotov cocktails and drug houses in the neighborhoods where we lived? And did all the people in John's neighborhood choose to live there? Could they have moved to Ventura and fit in? My respect for John Perkins and his family knew no bounds. But, incredibly, that respect would not translate into much action for years. It would take a move to Atlanta, Georgia, before things started to shift into high gear.

I've worked at two churches since moving to Atlanta in 1997. The first was a large mainline church in an affluent part of town. My brother Paul, after a brief Sunday morning visit, asked why the only black people on the property worked in the kitchen. I was embarrassed. I had been so excited about my new job there that I hadn't noticed. I mumbled some sort of excuse but again did nothing.

Fast-forward several years to my second job. I was (and am) on staff at Buckhead Church, the urban campus of North Point Ministries. Fairly early in my tenure here, two black men, who have since become my friends, approached me independently. They were both relatively new to Buckhead Church, which, at the time, was about 95 percent white. They both asked the same question: What does life at Buckhead Church look like for a black family? They weren't out to vilify Buckhead Church. They loved Andy Stanley's preaching. They just wondered if their wives and kids would fit in. I said that I didn't know, but I wanted to see what we could do. God's agenda for me in regard to disrupting racism began to shift into high gear.

Fast-forward once more to 2013. I was interviewing people for a full-time position on the Starting Point staff, a small department I headed up at Buckhead Church. Teesha McCrae (now Teesha Hadra) was the clear front-runner. We hired her, the first black woman to ever be hired on the full-time staff of Buckhead Church. She learned quickly and began to excel in her role. But something else was happening.

Over the next several months, Teesha and I developed a remarkable level of trust and respect. In my other role at Buckhead Church, director of staff development, I was working to create safe places for the church staff to have conversations about racial issues. Teesha became an invaluable partner in that regard. Like Bobby, she helped me see things from her perspective, which, among other things, is a black person's perspective. She helped me gauge when I might be pushing too hard and when I might not be pushing hard enough. The level of trust between us enabled me to ask some hard questions and allowed her to give some honest answers.

In the meantime, on the Starting Point side of things, Teesha and I were regularly interviewing potential volunteers to serve in that ministry. One afternoon we interviewed a white man named Fred

Hadra. He was perfect for the role. As it turns out, he and Teesha were also perfect for each other. They began to date. Several months later, Fred proposed to Teesha in the exact spot where they'd met: my office.

In February 2016, feeling almost like a family member, I had the honor of performing their wedding ceremony under a huge oak tree in a beautiful vineyard in central California. During that time, I met and got to know Teesha's family, further adding to my understanding and appreciation of what black people experience in the United States. When someone suggested I cowrite this book with a black person, I couldn't envision doing this with anyone other than Teesha.

As you can see from my story, I can't claim any moral high ground when it comes to working to disrupt racism. Quite the contrary, sometimes it feels like I should be disqualified from participating at all, because I took my sweet time getting involved. And I still don't have a lot of things figured out. But perhaps you see yourself in this. Perhaps you've had a handful of pivotal moments where you've clearly seen the need for God's people to get involved in the work of confronting racial injustice. Then, just like me, you've

> *I can't claim any moral high ground when it comes to working to disrupt racism. Quite the contrary, sometimes it feels like I should be disqualified.*

allowed years to pass by without doing much of anything. If that's you, don't worry. It's not too late to jump in. Consider letting the chapters that follow be your guide. You'll see that there's a lot to think about and a lot to do. At times it will be devilishly complicated. But one thing's certain: while the work will go on without you and me, it will go further and faster if we work together, both black and white.

DISCUSSION QUESTIONS

1. How old were you when you became aware of the presence of racial injustice in our country? How did that come about? How did it make you feel initially?

2. Did you grow up in a racially isolated context or in a racially diverse situation? In either case, how did this affect your thinking about people who didn't look like you?

3. How would you currently describe your relationships with people of different ethnic backgrounds? Would you say the diversity of your relationships is increasing, decreasing, or staying about the same?

4. John says that for him, becoming aware of racial injustice was a long, slow process. He mentions that it took even longer before he began to act on his awareness. How does this compare with your story? Why is it that for many white people, awareness of and work to disrupt racism can take a very long time?

Chapter Four

YOU'VE GOT TO BE KIDDING

Race prejudice . . . is a shadow over all of us, and the shadow is darkest over those who feel it least and allow its evil effects to go on.

—*Pearl S. Buck*

Race relations in the United States, both historically and at present, are characterized by grave injustice in the form of personal or individual racism. This type of racism involves person-to-person contact. It's in the comment that is rooted in racist stereotypes and in the use of racist slurs. Individual racism is also at play when one's deeply held beliefs of racial superiority erupt in verbal abuse or physical injury to a person or their property. In 1955, Emmett Till was lynched because a white woman said he had made flirtatious advances toward her. The woman later admitted to having fabricated that story. Emmett was only fourteen years old on the day he died. Two men, one of whom was the woman's husband, were charged with murder, tried in court, and acquitted by an all-white jury.[1] Emmett was murdered because he was black, and the men who killed him got away with it. The sense of injustice in this story is both palpable and undeniable. Even as a child, Emmett could not overcome the perceived threat that his blackness posed. Our history is riddled with the stories of many Emmett Tills and black people like him who lost their livelihoods, their dignity, and their very lives at the hands of white supremacists.

We may wish to believe that such instances of personal racism are a thing of the past. Some are tempted to argue that slavery and segregation have ended, so racism is no longer a reality. This is just not the case. According to the FBI's Uniform Crime Reporting Program in 2016, law enforcement agencies reported the occurrence of 6,121 hate crimes. Of these crimes, 57.5 percent involved bias due to race, ethnicity, or ancestry.[2] Statistics can make the problem of racism seem abstract, but behind each and every figure is a real person who experienced the all too real pain of racism. We want to share some of these real stories.

Phil, a black man, was born in the 1970s in a small town along the coast of South Carolina. The remnants of slavery were all around him. His family lived near the auction block where black people had been sold like cattle to the highest bidder to do grueling work on plantations. He walked by that auction block often, and each time, he was reminded of a history that seemed to seep into his present. Generations of people before him had felt the figurative and literal blows of racism. Both his grandfather and great-grandfather were terrorized and brutally murdered by white supremacists. No one was ever prosecuted for their deaths. Having tragically lost his father and grandfather, Phil's father carried a rage that infected every part of his life, a rage from which he has never seemed able to find freedom. Phil did not experience the care of a loving father.

He spent many years being angry at his father for both the rage he exhibited and for his absence from Phil's life. But the more of his family history Phil learned, the more he found a righteous anger caused by the pain that his father had witnessed and by all that he had lost because of racism.

Like generations of black people before him, Phil had firsthand experience of racism even as a child. When he was about eleven years old, he and his friends rode their bikes to the local country store to buy candy and play video games. Phil watched the store clerk treat the white customers with the cheer and kindness one would show to a longtime friend. However, when Phil or one of his black friends approached the counter, the warmth was gone. They were met with an icy glare. When the clerk handed Phil his change, she didn't place it in his hand. Instead, she dropped the money from several inches above the counter, causing the coins to fall everywhere. As he gathered the coins from the counter and bent over to pick the rest up off the floor, he knew that the clerk did not want to touch him. For him, it was clear that she perceived him as dirty or defective.

Phil continued to encounter white people who treated him as inferior. In high school, he was a star basketball player. During a game, a white player from the opposing team said, "Get off me, ni**er," as Phil was guarding him. Phil was so shocked by this blatant display of racism and vitriol that he froze.[3] It wasn't until his coach shouted from the sidelines, "Phil, get the ball," that he snapped out of it. Phil continued playing, but he couldn't forget what had happened. Later in the game, Phil encountered the same player at half court. This time, Phil reacted, and he pushed the white player. The referee called a technical foul against Phil. Phil explained to his coach what had happened, but his coach did not stand up for him. The coach took Phil out for the rest of the game, while the white player suffered no consequences. The white player had publicly degraded Phil, and his coach had abandoned him. Phil's combined experiences with race up to this point caused a deep distrust to take root within him. He didn't think he could trust a white coach again, so he chose to attend and play basketball for a historically black university.

After college, Phil was working as a personal trainer in Maryland. It was a bitterly cold Monday morning, so Phil was dressed warmly in black sweatpants and a black hoodie. Carrying his backpack as he always did, he walked the same route from his home to the bus stop on his way to work. When he got to the bus stop, he noticed a police officer parked nearby. He did not think much of it as it was not abnormal to see a police officer parked on the side of road. Maybe he was taking a break to have a little breakfast, Phil thought. He waited at that bus stop in his own neighborhood as he always did. After the scheduled arrival time for the bus came and went, Phil remembered that it was a government holiday, so the bus must have been running on a reduced schedule. Phil turned to go home to make other arrangements to get to work. Just as Phil turned to leave, the police officer slammed on the gas and sped away in the direction Phil was walking. Phil still did not think much of it. He was just going home after all. He thought the officer must be heading to an emergency call. As Phil kept walking, the officer sped toward the curb, nearly driving onto the sidewalk. The officer immediately jumped out of his car and yelled, "What are you doing? Let me see some ID." At this point, Phil's heart was racing out of fear and confusion. Phil told the officer that he lived in the neighborhood. The officer asked him for his address, and Phil promptly provided his ID. It turns out that someone had called the police because there was a "suspicious man" walking around the neighborhood whom they did not recognize. Phil asked the officer if he would have received the same treatment if he had been a white man walking through his neighborhood. The officer told Phil to have a nice day and left, abruptly ending their exchange.

Phil's neighbor arrogated to himself the power to determine who did and did not belong. As a black man, Phil fell into the latter category. Not only did Phil not belong, but he was also perceived as being suspicious and dangerous. This neighbor's assumptions were rooted in a racist stereotype of black men as criminal and dangerous. Phil's encounter with the police occurred in his own neighborhood while engaged in his normal routine of going to work. Imagine for a moment if these kinds of interactions with the police were a regular occurrence for you. There are many black men who do not have to imagine. Being confronted by police officers who have the power to take away their life and freedom in an instant and being treated as a guilty and dangerous person at the outset of each interaction are regular, sometimes daily occurrences. Many stories of black men and women killed by police make it onto the news. However, we are unlikely to hear about all of the times that a black man is stopped, questioned, and presumed guilty while engaging in the normal everyday things of life.

Racism is not only a part of the black *male* experience; black women are also singled out and discriminated against because of the color of their skin. There are complexities to living at the intersection of being black and female, complexities that are exacerbated in a world where whiteness and maleness function as the standard against which all else is measured. We won't address all those complexities here, but we will explore the experience of race for one black woman named Jasmine.

Jasmine grew up in a diverse middle-class town in Connecticut. Her hometown was something from a picture book. She spent winters skating on the local lake and skiing with friends and summers biking to the store to buy candy. Jasmine's first awareness of race occurred when she was about eight years old. She noticed that as more black and brown families moved into her neighborhood, white people moved out. She was not aware of the term *white flight* at the time and was unable to put words around what she was seeing. She just noticed that white people did not seem to want to live next to people who looked like her.

As Jasmine got older, her experience of being a black woman in America became more challenging. She had a close childhood friend, David. They did everything together. On one occasion, Jasmine was at David's house when his father came home from a get-together with his friends. David's mother asked her husband if he had enjoyed himself at the party. David's father replied, "It was great until this black guy showed up." Later, David's family invited her to their weekly Sunday dinner, which David's whole extended family attended. While everyone was sitting around the table, casually passing plates of food, David's grandmother said, "Who brought this black girl here?" In hearing these words from David's father and grandmother, Jasmine felt as though there was a spotlight shining directly on her, and yet she felt unseen and small.

> *Jasmine's experience taught her that for some white people, the very presence of black people caused animosity and a desire for separation.*

Whether it was in her neighborhood or around the dinner table, Jasmine's experience taught her that for some white people, the very presence of black people caused animosity and a desire for separation. It wasn't long after these incidents that Jasmine was called a "ni**er" for the first time.

Parents have a desire to shield their children from the harshest realities of the world for as long as possible. This is a privilege that is not afforded to black parents. The realities of race in America will be brought to bear on their children whether they like or not. It will undoubtedly be far too soon for their children to process fully.

Some people argue that racial injustice would just fade away if black people would stop focusing on or talking about race. There are many reasons why this argument does not hold up. One reason is that race and racism are regularly brought into the consciousness of black people through no action on their part. For example, when Jasmine was in high school, a group of students started a Young Republicans club. As their trademark, they had Confederate flags hanging out of their backpacks like a cape. These students were never asked to remove the flags. For Jasmine, this flag was a symbol of white supremacy and support for slavery. Yet, here were her classmates, miles away from any southern state, flying the Confederate flag proudly—it was in front of Jasmine every single day. She did not seek out racism or create racism by knowing the history of the Confederate flag. Racism was brought to her in a place that should have been safe.

> *Some people argue that racial injustice would just fade away if black people would stop focusing on or talking about race.*

As a black woman, Jasmine has also come face to face with the sinister effects of Eurocentric definitions of beauty. From this perspective, beauty is narrowly construed as including only those features that are associated with being of European descent, such as straight hair, lighter skin, and narrow noses. In contrast, curly/kinky hair, broader noses, and darker skin are outside the parameters of what is considered beautiful. From a young age, Jasmine encountered these white American beauty scripts—on television and in magazines edited by and aimed at white women. The messages did not stop when Jasmine became an adult. A white female coworker once told Jasmine that she was "the only pretty black person" she had ever seen, and she was so stunned by this discovery that she had to tell her boyfriend about it. What is the appropriate response to such a comment? To call it a backhanded compliment does not capture the comment's deep roots in the painful relegation of black physical traits to the category of ugly and unworthy. It was all backhand and no compliment. To be a black woman in America is to fight to be seen and valued precisely as God made you.

Jasmine and Phil's stories expose a malicious side of life in America. From childhood to adulthood and across the country, they were taught that their race rendered them dangerous and damaged in the eyes of some. Though their experiences are depressingly common, we still have reason to hope. Today, Phil pastors a multi-ethnic church in Southern California and is preparing to enter a PhD program in which his studies will center on the church's response to race and racism. Jasmine is a writer, performer, and filmmaker. She is also studying to be a mental health therapist. As a creative, she uses art to shine a light on racism, illuminating the problem in new ways. As a therapist, she heals the wounded. God is raising up people who will lead the church in participating in God's vision of reconciling all people to one another

> *God is raising up people who will lead the church in participating in God's vision of reconciling all people to one another and to God's self.*

and to God's self. Despite their experiences, Jasmine, Phil, and so many others like them have not given up. They have refused to allow the racism they have experienced to take root in their hearts and turn them into people they are not. They have recalled the people of all races who have loved them, supported them, and worked alongside them in the work of racial justice. We should not find ourselves hopeless in the face of their stories, even though they are painful. They remind us that racism is not in the past. It remains with us. Few black and brown people, if any, have remained untouched. What might happen if you made the space to listen to your friends' experiences of racism? How might both the sharer and the listener be changed and moved to action? These are just some of the questions that we will seek to answer throughout this book.

DISCUSSION QUESTIONS

1. Are you surprised by the number of hate crimes the FBI catalogued in the United States in 2016? Why or why not?

2. What part of Phil's story stands out for you? Are there any parts that you find surprising?

3. Do you think the interaction between Phil and the police officer by the bus stop is a rare or common event in the United States? In either case, is your tendency to "shrug it off" or be alarmed by such incidents?

4. What part of Jasmine's story stood out for you? Are there parts that you found surprising?

5. How do we maintain hope about the future of race relations in the United States in light of stories like those of Phil and Jasmine?

Chapter Five

RACISM ISN'T ALWAYS IN YOUR HEART

Our aim must be to create a world of fellowship and justice where no man's skin, color or religion, is held against him.

—Mary McLeod Bethune

We tend to think of racism as involving only a person's individual conduct. If asked to describe a racist, most people would picture a person wearing the white hood of the Ku Klux Klan, having the bald head of a skinhead, or having a swastika tattoo on her arm. We picture racists as those who hate and seek to inflict harm on people of color. They use racial epithets with a disturbing ease and frequency. They verbally harass people of color on the street, in restaurants, and in other establishments. Sometimes, their treatment of black people erupts in violence. This is personal racism, and it continues to be a very real problem. In chapter 4 we shared the stories of some of our friends who had experienced personal racism.

But personal racism is not the only form racism can take. It isn't the whole picture of racism and it never has been, because racism isn't always in your heart—sometimes it's in your legal codes, in your banks' lending policies, in the geography of your county's polling places.

With personal racism, the individual is at the center of the problem. But there is another kind of racism, where whole institutions are at the center of the problem. Racism is embedded in our culture, values, expectations, laws, and institutions. In other words, racism is structural and systemic. Systemic racism refers to the various ways that laws, policies, procedures, and values act on institutions in complex ways to discriminate against and disadvantage particular groups of people. And nice, well-meaning, church-going people can passively, even unknowingly, cooperate with institutions that are infected with systemic racism, thereby passively participating in those systems. Well-meaning white people can have black friends, marry black partners, or raise black children—all while inadvertently *benefiting from* the systems that disadvantage black people.

One of the many problems with systemic racism is that its sinister subtlety makes it hard to discern. But it is there, and it can be discovered—indeed, the empirical evidence showing that systemic racism exists is readily available.

> *Racism is embedded in our culture, values, expectations, laws, and institutions. In other words, racism is structural and systemic.*

Some people believe because slavery has ended that segregation is no longer the law of the land, that black people no longer live under the Jim Crow laws of the late nineteenth century, and that racism no longer affects the everyday lives of black people. The reality is that the impact of racial injustice continues in our country in the form of systemic and structural racism. In this chapter, we will look at examples of systemic racism in housing, education, and the criminal justice system. These examples are by no means exhaustive, but we have chosen these areas because of their centrality to economic security, and in the case of the criminal justice system, one's very freedom.

In his book *The Color of Law*, Richard Rothstein argues that explicitly racist government policies that historically segregated neighborhoods laid the groundwork for current systems that maintain racially segregated neighborhoods. From the Great Depression in the 1930s up to the 1950s, middle- and working-class white and black families experienced a severe housing shortage. In response, as part of the New Deal, Franklin D. Roosevelt created America's first public housing facilities for people who were not part of the war effort.[1] However, black Americans were either relegated to segregated buildings or were excluded from public housing altogether. Other economic development and jobs programs that were part of the New Deal were similarly structured to reinforce segregation and economically disadvantage black Americans. This landscape of segregated housing and racially discriminatory policies meant that black Americans were consigned to high-rise buildings that hindered

> *Well-meaning white people can have black friends, marry black partners, or raise black children— all while inadvertently benefiting from the systems that disadvantage black people.*

community life, in neighborhoods where access to jobs and social services were more difficult and community policing was an impossibility.[2]

The practice of segregating public housing has not abated since the 1950s and 1960s. Though federal and local governments may have eliminated laws that expressly discriminate along racial lines, their practices function in ways that accomplish the same end. Most cities continue to situate public housing buildings in predominantly minority and low-income areas. Federal subsidies for low-income housing are mainly used to assist with rent payments in apartments in segregated, predominantly minority neighborhoods, where economic opportunities are limited. Public housing tenants are almost always segregated by race, and facilities that are predominantly occupied by white tenants have better amenities, services, and maintenance than facilities predominantly occupied by black tenants.[3]

Systemic racism is not unique to public housing. It is also embedded in the private housing market. In the 1930s, after the Great Depression, the federal government needed to assess the risk associated with providing home loans to reduce lenders' risk. Thus, the Roosevelt administration created the Home Owner's Loan Corporation (HOLC). In a practice that came to be known as "redlining," the HOLC graded the risk of neighborhoods based almost entirely on their racial makeup. If black people lived in a neighborhood, even if it was solidly middle class, it was shaded red on a map, which indicated the highest level of risk in lending. This risk was based on an unsubstantiated belief that black Americans were more likely to default on their loans and that the presence of black people in a neighborhood lowered the property values of white-owned homes in the area. When the Federal Housing Administration (FHA) was created in 1934, it insured mortgages that covered 80 percent of the purchase price. Such a guarantee from the FHA could place home ownership within reach for many Americans, but black Americans were once again excluded as the FHA viewed home loans in predominantly black, or even racially mixed, neighborhoods to be too risky to insure.[4]

Many neighborhoods still bear the marks of redlining. In 1941, a New Jersey real estate agent tried to sell homes in a new suburban development called Fanwood to twelve black Americans, all of whom had good credit. Banks would not issue mortgages to them without FHA approval, which the agency declined to give because of their race. Today, the population of Fanwood is only 5 percent black in a county where the black population is 25 percent.[5] Black Americans were judged as poor financial risks, placing homeownership out of reach for many black families at a time when home ownership made economic growth and wealth accumulation possible for much of white America.[6]

Home ownership remains elusive for many black Americans even today. A lovely black couple from our church, like many newly-weds, was trying to buy their first home. Since being pre-approved for a mortgage, they have been on the hunt for the "perfect" house. But they've noticed something unsettling in their search. Very few homes in Atlanta's predominantly black neighborhoods are for sale. It also happens that these are the

When home ownership is systemically taken off the table for black Americans, the effects reverberate for generations to come.

very neighborhoods that are within their budget. It turns out that a house for sale in south DeKalb County, one of metro-Atlanta's largest municipalities, might sell for half the going rate found in north DeKalb County.[7] By the way, north DeKalb County is primarily white; south DeKalb County is primarily black.

A *Washington Post* analysis found that the more black people who reside in a particular zip code, the worse that zip code's housing values have done since the most recent housing crisis in 2008. Home values in predominantly black neighborhoods have been the least likely to recover.[8] As home values decline, so do property values, which are used to fund schools and services. In a vicious cycle, the decline in the quality of schools and services only drives property values down further. The economic status of one's parents is a strong predictor of the next generation's economic status. When home ownership is systemically taken off the table for black Americans, the effects reverberate for generations to come. Today, the median income for white families is about $60,000, while the median income for black families is about $37,000. The figures for household wealth are even more stark. The median household wealth for white families is about $134,000, while the median household wealth for black families is $11,000.[9] While many white working- and middle-class Americans have enjoyed appreciating property values and an attendant accumulation of wealth that can then be passed on to subsequent generations, many black families have suffered under the cumulative impact of generations of systemic racism in housing and lending practices.

Even accumulation of wealth does not make black people immune from the effects of systemic racism. Most white boys raised in wealthy families will remain wealthy as adults, but black boys in similarly wealthy households are more likely to become poor as adults.[10] These disparities persist even when black and white boys grow up in families with similar family structures and levels of education.[11] It seems that for black men, in particular, escaping the impact of systemic racism is a difficult if not impossible feat.

Like housing practices, the public education system in America is plagued by systemic racism. Racial segregation in public schools may have been outlawed, but black children in America have not yet gained equal access to quality education. In the 1954 case of *Brown v. Board of Education*, the Supreme Court of the United States ruled that racial segregation of children in public schools was unconstitutional. However, schools today are more segregated than they were forty years ago, in large part because neighborhoods remain segregated.[12] Some school districts have not only failed to reject the "separate but equal doctrine" as mandated by the Brown decision; they have enacted a separate and unequal doctrine in their educational systems.[13] Not only are schools racially segregated, but students of color attend schools that are underfunded and under-resourced as compared to their white counterparts. Attending desegregated schools leads to higher achievement of black students— not because learning alongside white children inherently increases the value of education. The higher achievement is likely attributable to the additional resources and better facilities that are available where white children attend schools in larger numbers.[14] Even those schools that may be labeled "desegregated" because of their overall racial composition remain internally segregated because of ability tracks that reflect racial bias.[15] The potential for a quality education to trans-

> *Racial segregation in public schools may have been outlawed, but black children in America have not yet gained equal access to quality education.*

form children's lives cannot be overstated. Education is linked to higher income, better employment opportunities, and even better health.[16] All of these benefits are withheld from many black children due to the systemic racism that shapes the educational system in America.

Let's turn now to the final locus of systemic racism that we will examine: the criminal justice system. Following the start of the War on Drugs, which was instituted at a time when rates of drug offenses were on the decline, we saw the rates of incarceration balloon to unprecedented levels. Between 1980 and 2000, the number of people incarcerated in the United States increased from 300,000 to more than 2 million. We have the highest rates of incarceration in the world, far surpassing even countries with more restrictive systems of government like Russia, Iran, and China.[17]

That racism is a component of American rates of incarceration is difficult to deny. Black Americans are incarcerated in state prisons at

> *The personal impact of arrest and conviction for crime cannot be overstated. In many states, it means losing the right to vote forever, not to mention the impact on the ability to secure employment, housing, and government assistance.*

five times the rate of white people. Thirty-eight percent of state prisoners are black although they make up 13 percent of the general population.[18] No other country imprisons as many of its racial and ethnic minorities as does the United States.[19] In Washington, DC, for example, some estimate that three out of four young black men can expect to spend time in prison. These rates are not unlike those in other areas of the United States. It may surprise some to know that these racial disparities in incarceration rates cannot be explained by more criminality among black people. People of all racial backgrounds use and sell drugs at very similar rates. There is evidence to suggest that white people are actually more likely to engage in drug crimes than people of color.[20] The personal impact of arrest and conviction for crime cannot be overstated. In many states, it means losing the right to vote forever, not to mention the impact on the ability to secure employment, housing, and government assistance.

None of these examples are a secret. Books, podcasts, magazine articles, TED Talks, and blogs documenting past and current examples of systemic racism are readily available. For some people, pausing to learn (or relearn) the painful history of the treatment of black people in this country and how that history continues to affect the lives of black people today is the next step.

Some may think that systemic racism is a novel idea invented by "social justice warriors" or "liberals." The truth is that systemic injustice is not new, and dismantling it has always been part of the work God is doing in the world. Take the Book of Amos, for example. The prophecies in Amos were given at a time when Israel enjoyed great economic prosperity and peace. Through Amos, God exposed Israel's participation in social and economic injustice among its own people. God first denounced Israel's practice of selling the innocent poor into slavery (Amos 2:6). This verse refers to the practice of corrupt courts colluding with the wealthy to bring poor people into court and levy fines against them. Because the poor are unable to pay the fine, they are sold into slavery.[21] Thus, God decried a judicial system that denied justice to the poor. God also said in Amos 2:7 that Israel had "trample[d] the head of the poor" into the dirt and, as one commentator put it, "they keep the oppressed from getting anywhere."[22] This is the context for the words made famous by Martin Luther King Jr. that are found in Amos 5:24: "But let justice roll down like waters, and righteousness like an ever-flowing stream." These words are God's cry to a nation whose judicial and economic systems oppress the poor and the powerless. God is clear about what is required of Israel. God does not desire or delight in their festivals, "solemn assemblies," burnt offerings on the altar, or songs of worship (Amos 5:21-23). God expects Israel to enact justice so much so that it flows like a stream that goes on forever, sustaining life and allowing humanity to flourish. God continued this work through Jesus, who, drawing on the words of the prophet Isaiah, said that He had come to "let the oppressed go free" (Luke 4:18 NRSV). To follow Jesus is to free the oppressed. To follow Jesus is to enact justice. So those who follow Jesus must engage with God in the work of disrupting racism, both personal and systemic.

If Christians are going to disrupt racism, we will need to think more carefully about core American values. For example, the American Dream suggests that as long as you work hard, you can achieve anything. Embedded in this idea is a strong commitment to individual choice. However, this version of the American Dream ignores the ways that the power of individual choice is compromised when individuals live and work in unjust systems. If the organizing political and economic realities of your community are unjust, you might work hard and make good choices, but your life may not get better. Unjust systems move the

> *If Christians are going to disrupt racism, we will need to think more carefully about core American values.*

American Dream out of reach. And when the injustice of a system is organized along racist lines, it moves the American Dream out of the reach of black Americans. What is a reality for white Americans becomes a myth for their black counterparts.

To be clear, we are not trying to devalue hard work or to imply that personal choices have no impact on one's life outcomes. What we are saying is that there is another force at work that affects the lives of people of color regardless of the choices they make. That force is systemic racism. Put bluntly, systemic racism gives white people an unfair advantage. This is called *white privilege*. This phrase may make you bristle, but stick with us on this one. The term *privilege* does not refer to a person's wealth. That a white person has privilege does not mean that they will never be poor, will never suffer, will never be fired from a job, or will never end up in jail. Privilege just means that if a white person encounters these life events, more than likely it will not be because of the color of their skin. White people have privilege because they have social, political, and economic advantages in society. At the very least, white privilege means not being subject to the centuries-long effects of systemic racism that continue to affect the lives of black people.

Antiracism scholar Peggy McIntosh defines white privilege as "an invisible package of unearned assets which [she] can count on cashing in each day, but about which [she] was meant to remain oblivious."[23] It is the obliviousness that seems to most concern McIntosh. Discovering the "unseen dimensions" of one's privilege or advantage is a necessary first step in any effort to reform racist systems.[24] Thus, McIntosh has developed an inventory to help white people see where white privilege may have shaped their lives in ways they had not realized. Her inventory asks whether the person taking the inventory can affirm statements like "I can if I wish arrange to be in the company of people of my race most of the time" and "I can turn on the television or open to the front page of the paper and see people of my race widely represented."[25] Seeing your own group widely represented on TV and knowing you can be around people of your own racial group (at church, at work, at the airport)—these are the kinds of invisible unearned assets that constitute white privilege. (Indeed, never having to notice, until an inventory points it out, that most of the people on the front page of the paper look like you is itself a marker of white privilege.) The items on McIntosh's inventory expose an environment that is calibrated for white people. The implicit message of the items on her inventory is "to be white is the norm, the standard." The seemingly "soft" things on McIntosh's inventory are the legacy of long-standing racist systems in America. They are not equivalent to segregation or slavery, but they are the remnants of those systems.

The twin forces of systemic racism and white privilege are a lot to think about. Discomfort with these ideas can cause white people to withdraw from conversations about racism, which serves only to protect these racist systems. But recognition of systemic racism and white privilege can also motivate white people to take action. If you have a role in the problem, you can have a role in the solution. The first step to being part of the solution is to enter into a relationship with someone who is different from you. In the context of that relationship, you'll start to see things from your friend's point of view (and he or she from yours).

> **The first step to being part of the solution is to enter into a relationship with someone who is different from you.**

Over time, you and your friend will be able to participate in the tricky but essential work of challenging systemic racism in your workplace, your church, your city, your business, and in all the places where you have influence and power. This is our challenge. This is our opportunity. This is part of God's work in the world.

DISCUSSION QUESTIONS

Because systemic racism can be a new and/or controversial idea for some, the following is an expanded set of discussion questions. This can help facilitate a more rigorous exploration of the ideas contained in this chapter.

1. Somehow, not indulging in personal racism became the upper limit of Americans' obligation to one another; that is, we often think that if we do not injure people's bodies, feelings, or property because of the color of their skin, we do not contribute to the problem of racism in America. If we do not harbor personally racist feelings or engage in personally racist acts, we could not possibly be part of the problem, or so some people think. Why has eradicating or abjuring personal racism become, for many people, the only goal?

2. Our country is made up of more than 300 million people. Each of these people participates in an endless number of groupings and affiliations. There are book clubs and gangs, political parties and Little League teams. There are people who live inside the city limits of Chicago and people who are members of church choirs; people over thirty and people who served time in prison. To be human is to be part of a group with whom you share some sort of common experience or affiliation. Name three groups of which you are a part.

3. Each of these groupings has its own system or way of doing things. Some of these systems are explicit, like banks that have very specific, documented rules for determining the financial qualifications of those to whom they lend money. Sometimes these systems are implicit, like the dance club that admits only people whom the bouncers deem to be "cool." Do you think every group has both explicit and implicit systems for doing what they do?

4. Just like individuals, groups of people are prone to various types of systemic dysfunction. Sometimes these dysfunctions are purely performance related. For example, a college football team may not have an effective offensive line. However, sometimes these dysfunctions are moral in nature. For example, a few years ago, a European car maker created an electronic system that enabled its automobiles to falsify the results of their emissions tests. What are some other examples of systemic dysfunction? Do you think systemic dysfunction tends to exist more in the explicit or implicit systems that govern the way a group works?

5. The term *systemic racism* refers to a moral dysfunction within the systems of a group or organization that results in the unjust treatment of certain ethnic groups. John and Teesha cited the disproportionate percentage of black people who are incarcerated in the United States as an example of systemic racism. Do you think this is a good example of systemic racism? Why or why not?

6. Systemic racism is inherently immoral but doesn't always start off being illegal. For example, the systemic racism that interfered with black people voting was always immoral but was not illegal until laws were passed making it so. When should a country pass laws against systemic racism?

7. When certain types of systemic racism remain legal with no apparent prospect for a legal remedy, what are some alternate strategies that can be brought to bear to disrupt that kind of racism?

8. Visit www.nationalseedproject.org to take Peggy McIntosh's white privilege inventory. Discuss the results. What did you find surprising?

Chapter Six

RISKY BUSINESS

Fortune sides with him who dares.

—Virgil

R ecently, students at the seminary where I (Teesha) am earning
a master of divinity engaged in a silent protest over issues
of racial injustice at our baccalaureate ceremony, which precedes
graduation. We protested because, among other things, there were
too few black faculty members, too few black administrators, and too
few black authors listed in course syllabi. After baccalaureate, a friend
and classmate, Luke, asked me to grab coffee and discuss the protest.
Almost immediately I had a sense of dread, but not because I don't
like Luke. Both my husband and I have immense care and respect for
Luke and his wife. I had a sense of dread because Luke is not only of
a different race but also of a different nationality. I feared that these
two layers of difference would make any conversation about race

71

exceedingly difficult. I would have to unpack the unique complexities of how race plays out in my American context. Luke is also a very intelligent and analytical person, so I knew there would be no softball questions. We were going to go deep. It was also an extremely busy season. I was swamped with school, writing, work, being a wife, and trying to navigate this post-protest world on my campus with other black students and interested parties. To be honest, I was not looking forward to this coffee.

For people of color, building friendships with people who are different from us can be risky business. Add in the extra layer of talking about race, and you might just prefer to run in the other direction. These risks are not imagined. They are very real. In cross-racial relationships, I am sometimes concerned that someone is going to say something harmful, offensive, or just downright racist. It's not so much that I worry that someone is going to use a racial epithet to refer to me in the middle of our conversation. It's more the tacitly prejudiced comment that gives me pause. I was once talking to a friend who was telling the story of a recent encounter she had at the grocery store. At the center of the story was a "big scary black man." My friend actually referred to him in that way, and it seemed utterly normal for her to do so. She didn't trip over these words or exhibit any sense that perhaps her words reflected a racial bias. She was just describing the characters in her story. That's it, at least from her perspective. What she didn't realize was that she was falling into a centuries-old stereotype of black men as inherently violent and dangerous. This stereotypical view of black men had become so much a part of her psyche that she saw no problem with holding on to that stereotype and then expressing it out loud.

Because I have a lot of white colleagues and friends, this happens a lot. When it does, I have two choices. I can either call out my friend by telling her that she was furthering an old racist stereotype, or I can decide that it's a been a long day and I just don't have the energy for battle. Black and brown people who live or work in predominantly white spaces or who choose to be in community with people who look different from them face this choice often.

When you have had a few of these encounters, you start to become guarded in cross-racial relationships. I start to wonder if it is safe to share all of my thoughts, feelings, and experiences with people who look different from me. I find myself asking, "Can I trust this person?" The risk here is discovering that someone I cared for, respected, and thought I knew was never interested in fully knowing me. They wanted to be friends with a facade of the real me. They were content to let the fact that I was black just rest on the surface of our relationship rather than exploring how my race affects my daily life and perhaps theirs as well. The thought of "I have black friends" can sometimes obscure the fact that they are holding themselves apart from the hard work of understanding my experience and the role racism plays in our culture.

Every once in a while, I find a safe space in cross-racial friendships, a place where I can speak freely. But then there is the pressure that my friend expects me to be a spokesperson for the entire black community. The experiences of black people in America are diverse and complex. We can look at data and try to draw some conclusions about the broad experience of black people. However, numbers should never be used to obscure the unique experiences of real people. It is nearly impossible for me to speak for all black people in all times and places; but sometimes white friends place that burden on me, especially if I am their only black friend.

What I can do is share my own experiences and how I have come to make sense of those experiences in my own unique context. I share those experiences for the purpose of building a deep and authentic friendship, not to convince my white friends that racism exists. The latter cannot be the purpose of cross-racial relationships. The fact is, I don't want to be a tutor. I want to be a friend. Learning about how race has played out in America is good and necessary. Just don't mistake a coffee shop for a classroom.

Finally, when I walk into conversations with white friends, I am afraid I will discover that my empathy is much more limited than I would like to believe. As a black Christian, I would like to think that I can show an unlimited amount of empathy toward those who are different from me. I am so often on the outside that I should be uniquely equipped to listen to the diverse experiences of others. I should be able to see things from another's perspective. The truth is, I have not found this to be case. I can't always see things from another person's perspective—and sometimes, frankly, I don't really want to.

I was having lunch with a white acquaintance recently who mentioned listening to a sermon by a pastor who I knew had been vocal about his negative views on immigration and his view that addressing issues of racial justice were not relevant to the gospel. The mere mention of this pastor shut me down. I made all kinds of assumptions about my lunch partner. I assumed she was narrow-minded and uninformed. I wondered what opinions she shared with this pastor. What did she *really* think about my immigrant parents and my black skin? It was hard to remain plugged into the conversation after that. It became difficult to care about and take on her perspective. In other words, I discovered that there were limits to my empathy.

My post-baccalaureate coffee with Luke was not easy, either, but it was worth all the occasional moments of awkwardness—not because we solved all the problems of the world, but because amid the discomfort, we laughed and we prayed. We prayed for our seminary, for our classmates, and for the country. Friendships with people who are different can be challenging and even complex. But if you discover that you are in such a relationship and yet no risk is involved, then perhaps it's not the kind of friendship we're asking you to consider in this book. So, take heart! If the friendship in which you find yourself feels a little scary, then you're probably in the right place. Don't give up. You're doing exactly what love demands.

DISCUSSION QUESTIONS

1. Why does Teesha feel that building friendships with people who don't look like her is sometimes risky?

2. It is suggested that at times white people unconsciously perpetuate racial stereotypes. The idea of portraying black men as inherently violent and dangerous serves as an example. As you think about this, what other stereotypes come to mind?

3. Do you think there is a difference between racism and insensitivity to racial issues? If so, how would you describe that difference?

4. Sometimes black people feel like their white friends are more interested in using them as a source of information about racism than they are in getting to know them as unique individuals. How might a white person make sure that doesn't happen?

5. Teesha mentions that at times friendships with people who don't look like her reveal a certain lack of empathy on her part. How does one (whether white or black) acquire a growing sense of empathy?

Chapter Seven

WHITE FEAR

What people resist is not change per se, but loss.

—*Ronald Heifetz*

I (John) took my first class in psychology when I was a junior in high school. It was there that I learned about the fight-or-flight syndrome. If you took a psychology class somewhere along the way, you probably learned about that too. Put simply, it says that when we are afraid of something, we tend to either run away from it or attack it. It's somewhat surprising that the same stimulus can produce such opposite behaviors. When it comes to talking about racism in this country, there is a lot of running away and attacking.

This is a big problem. If we're afraid to talk about racism with people, especially people who don't look like us, we'll either avoid the conversations altogether or we'll switch to attack mode (sometimes subtly, sometimes not so subtly) once the conversation has started. In either case, fear robs us of a tremendous opportunity. In the meantime, the stories about racial injustice continue to pile up. Tensions rise and polarization continues. The good news is that it's never too late to change. But the longer we allow fear to hold us hostage, the longer it will take to see things start to turn around. So, if we want to disrupt racism, we need to disrupt the fear that prevents us from talking about it.

Now it's true that not everybody is afraid to talk about racism. You might be one of those people who's moved past that. It's also true that other people switch to "fight mode" when they talk about racism not because they are afraid but because they are angry. We'll talk more about that in chapter 8. In the meantime,

> *If we want to disrupt racism, we need to disrupt the fear that prevents us from talking about it.*

we'll focus on how to deal with the fear that makes it hard to talk about racism or even to engage with people who don't look like us.

It turns out that fear is virtually impossible to conquer until we're clear about exactly what it is we're afraid of. And it also turns out that black people and white people are afraid of different things when it comes to conversations about race and racism. So, we'll begin by identifying some things that white people fear. Then we'll move to the next chapter, where we'll look at some things that black people deal with. Our hope is that once black people know what white people are afraid of and vice versa, we might be able to help each other out. So, get ready. This may get a little personal. It might even get a little painful. But it will be a good pain, the kind of pain that accompanies healing.

When we start to consider the fears white people have about discussing race and racism, some people might ask, "What on earth do white people have to be afraid of? They're not the ones that have been kidnapped, enslaved, marginalized, dehumanized, Jim Crowed, and abused over the centuries." That's a legitimate point of view. For example, there is no museum in the United States to commemorate the racially motivated lynching of white people. This is because the racially motivated lynching of white people has hardly ever happened.[1] On the other hand, more than four thousand black people have been lynched for racial reasons. These lynchings have been documented and referenced at the National Memorial for Peace and Justice in Montgomery, Alabama. It is nicknamed the "Lynching Memorial." Considering these facts of our history, it is tempting to look askance at the idea of white people being afraid to talk about this. But it's just this history that leads some white people to fear talking about race and racism. They are aware of the horrible history of racism in our country, and because of that awareness, they feel ashamed or feel they are being blamed when the topic of racism comes up.

Maybe those fears are warranted. Maybe they aren't. But unaddressed, those fears will continue to disrupt our efforts to disrupt racism.

So, let's dive in. What exactly *are* white people afraid of? There is a lot of research that tries to answer that question at a sociological

> *"What on earth do white people have to be afraid of?"*

level. But our interests in this chapter are more of an interpersonal nature. We've had hundreds of conversations about race and racism with white people. As we thought about those conversations, certain themes began to appear. To properly cover them all would take a whole separate book. For now, we'll focus on just three: White people are afraid of offending black people. They are afraid of making black people angry. And finally, white people are afraid of the discomfort they will likely feel as they discuss racism with someone who doesn't look like them.

When I moved to Atlanta, I had my first conversation with a black man in the South about race and racism. The man's name was Theron Nixon. Theron, along with his family, had started to attend Buckhead Church, where I am one of the pastors. This was in 2008, when Buckhead Church was an almost entirely white congregation. Theron had some important questions he wanted to discuss. What would it look like for a black family to fully enter the life of Buckhead Church? How would he and his wife feel if they joined one of the many small groups that Buckhead Church maintained? How would his kids feel about participating in Waumba Land and UpStreet, the preschool and grade school ministries there? Theron wondered if he and his family would feel welcomed and included. It was and is a valid question.

As I reflected on my conversation with Theron, I was able to identify some things I was afraid of. The first thing I feared was offending Theron. You'll remember that I am from Southern California, where racism plays out very differently than it does in Atlanta, Georgia. Because I was still in the early stages of learning about how things work in the South, I was afraid that, in my ignorance, I would say something that Theron would find offensive. For example, I didn't know if I should use the term *black* or *African American*. What if I said the wrong thing? You'll notice that throughout this book we pretty much use the word *black*. You'll see why in chapter 17.

The next fear on my shortlist is a little awkward to talk about. It's also complicated because it involves what arguably might be called a racial stereotype. But this particular fear lurks in the mind of a lot of white people, and it briefly crossed my mind as I was preparing to meet with Theron: What if Theron becomes angry during our conversation?

Racism is a painful issue. I worried that I might inadvertently say something that would make Theron angry. I didn't really know him at that point. I didn't know his story. Was there a specific issue within the vast topic of racism that was particularly painful for him? The possibility of unintentionally provoking Theron's anger scared me.

Because white people are afraid of angering their black interlocutors, a lot of white people won't risk talking to black people about racial issues. This fear is not entirely unjustified. Sometimes anger is a reasonable response to racism. White people must learn to make some space for black people to be angry. We'll talk more about this in chapter 8. But for now, we must acknowledge that the fear of provoking anger has drastically reduced the number of conversations about race between white and black people. As a result, the work of disrupting racism has itself been disrupted.

> *Sometimes anger is a reasonable response to racism. White people must learn to make some space for black people to be angry.*

The final thing I feared as I entered into the conversation with Theron was my own discomfort. Even if I didn't offend Theron, even if Theron didn't get mad, I was afraid the conversation would just be plain old awkward. Indeed, conversations between white and black people about issues of race and racism will almost always start off with a certain level of discomfort. How could they not? Perhaps the discomfort of white people is a sign that they're actually engaging in the issue before them.

This doesn't mean that the discomfort is chronic. As a friendship starts to emerge, trust builds and discomfort diminishes. Of course, in a real friendship, conversations about race will be interspersed with conversations about whatever shared interests there are. If a black person and a white person never talk about football or music or food or faith or whatever it is that they hold in common, then they don't have a friendship. And without a friendship, the conversations about race will slowly cease because the relationship will dissolve. Friendship is the glue that can hold white and black people together and provide a context within which conversations about racism can occur. But like we said, these conversations usually start off being somewhat uncomfortable.

This is a problem because we love to be comfortable. Cumulatively speaking, we spend vast amounts of money on our comfort. We create physical, emotional, and relational "comfort zones" where we feel safe and secure. In principle, there's nothing wrong with this—we need places and people where we can let down our guard and relax, where we can experience rest and recuperation. But if I insist on turning my comfort zone from a place I occasionally visit into a place where I hide, then I will miss the best part of my life. I will never experience the best version of myself there. It's the tension and challenge I experience outside my comfort zone that God uses to form and shape me. Nobody's life changes for the better when we value comfort over character. When we make comfort

> *If a black person and a white person never talk about football or music or food or faith or whatever it is that they hold in common, then they don't have a friendship.*

our ultimate value, our comfort zone ceases to be a place where we rest and becomes a prison where we rot, separated from what God wants to do in us and through us.

I want to point out one more thing about my meeting with Theron: the unflagging grace he brought to our conversation. He didn't coddle me, but neither did he make the conversation more difficult. He reminded me of some things Desmond Tutu said in his book *No Future Without Forgiveness*. In that book, Bishop Tutu reflects on the gut-wrenchingly difficult task the black people of South Africa faced in forgiving the white people of that country who had endorsed and maintained the horrible, state-sponsored reign of apartheid. At one point he writes,

> Peace is possible, especially if today's adversaries were to imagine themselves becoming friends and begin acting in ways that would promote such a friendship developing in reality. It would be wonderful if, as they negotiate, they tried to find ways of accommodating each other's needs. A readiness to make concessions is a sign of strength, not weakness. And it can be worthwhile sometimes to lose a battle in order in the end to win the war.[2]

Tutu's approach seems outrageous. It is countercultural. On a human level, it makes no sense, yet it smacks of the gospel of Jesus Christ. And it has created significant change in South Africa. It doesn't diminish or dismiss the horrors of apartheid even one little bit. But it has made a way for a country to cease to be held hostage by those horrors. I experienced this on a smaller scale with Theron when we met for the first time all those years ago. Since then he has become a friend. Together we are working to disrupt racism.

So, here's where we are. When it comes to talking about racism with black people or with any person of color, we white people are often afraid of offending our conversation partner. We are afraid we might make him or her angry. And we tend to be afraid of the discomfort that inevitably surrounds these conversations. If you are a white person reading this and you're wondering what to do, there's one thing that won't work. It won't help to try and wait until these fears dissipate. Waiting never dissipates fear. Action does. When Jesus tells us not to be afraid (see John 14:27), the best way to obey this imperative isn't to ask God to take away your fear. Instead, ask God to give you courage to act in spite of your fear. As you lean into the courage God gives, you'll discover that the fear slowly begins to subside. That's the way it works. But don't take our word for it. Try it out—and the sooner the better.

> *Waiting never dissipates fear. Action does.*

DISCUSSION QUESTIONS

1. Have you had conversations about race or racism with a person from a different racial background than yours? How did those conversations go? Do you feel like the benefits of the conversation were worth the effort?

2. If you're a white person, do you resonate with the fears John describes in this chapter? If you're a black person, is there anything John mentions that you find surprising?

3. It is pointed out in this chapter that there is sometimes a temptation to critique the legitimacy of white people's fears when it comes to discussing racism. Why is that temptation a problem? Why might critiquing their fears be unhelpful?

4. Have you ever made a person who doesn't look like you angry or frustrated during a conversation about racial issues? What happened? How did the conversation conclude? If you could ask a person of a different race one question, what would you ask?

Chapter Eight

ANGER

Is it right for you to be angry?

—God (NIV)

If you are from the South, live in the South, or have ever driven through the South, you've probably heard of kudzu. Kudzu is a green, leafy vine that grows everywhere. It often covers the steep hills along a roadway or railroad. It snakes up and around tree trunks and telephone poles until the leaves are all you can see. You can find it covering the side of an abandoned house or overtaking an untended backyard. Horticulturists call it an invasive species, which means that it thrives outside of its normal habitat and spreads aggressively. In favorable conditions, it can grow about a foot per day. Kudzu can be so difficult to get rid of that some savvy homeowners and municipalities have taken to enlisting the help of goats to eat the kudzu. Getting rid of it requires steady and continuous attention. Wherever kudzu grows, it drapes the landscape like a veil, covering every nook and cranny, traversing every curve with ease. The veil of kudzu can be so thick that it shuts out all the sunlight, killing the underlying vegetation.

In conversations with people who are different from us, anger is like kudzu. As we approach topics of race and culture, anger can grow and spread very quickly, overtaking every part of the conversation. Once anger enters the conversation, it covers everything until you can no longer see what lies beneath it. Anger obscures the true meaning of our words. We can't hear or comprehend well when we are angry. Under these conditions, we are likely to miss what our friends are saying. When we cannot hear the other person's story or perspective, we cannot see it either. We become more concerned about making our next point than about listening or attending to the needs of our friend. Sometimes, anger can be so thick that a person's humanity becomes obscured. Anger causes us to value whatever point we're trying to make more than we value the other's personhood.

As we contemplate entering into relationships with people who do not look like us, we have to ask ourselves the question God asked Jonah in Jonah 4:4 (NIV), "Is it right for you to be angry?"

> *When we cannot hear the other person's story or perspective, we cannot see it either.*

For some people, the clear answer to this question is yes. There is such a thing as righteous anger. It is right to be angry in the face of injustice. We are angry every time we watch yet another cell phone video of a black man being gunned down by the police. We are angry when a white person discovers that a black person hates her because she is white. We are angry when we read another news story about the police being called on black people for engaging in everyday tasks like sitting in a coffee shop, taking a nap in their college dormitory's common area, or having a barbecue in the park. Then there is the anger that results from being rejected, belittled, or harmed because of your race. It is normal and perhaps healthy to be angry when things are not as they should be for us or for our neighbors. Anger can arise out of our empathy and serve as a sign that we are paying attention to the pain of our friends and neighbors. Righteous anger is not opposed to love; it is an expression of love. It says, "I love you too much to be unaffected by your pain." Righteous anger can catalyze our faith. In the face of injustice, anger can move us from inaction to direct engagement. Such anger is healthy precisely because it is not an end in and of itself and can function to restore shalom.[1] It can be God's way of issuing a call to action.

Righteous anger has its place in the Christian life, but it is not without potential pitfalls. Experiencing anger is kind of like making a hardboiled egg. The egg is submerged in boiling water, and it's even getting tossed around a bit. The heat is causing the egg to cook. The heat is both good and necessary. But we've all walked away from a boiling egg only to come back and find that the water has boiled over. The heat cooks the egg, but it can still cause the water to boil over and make a mess. So even righteous anger requires your attention. Otherwise, what is good and holy might just devolve into bitterness and defensiveness. Let's look at two complementary commitments to help guard against this: be open and practice nonjudgmental listening.

Being open means sharing your righteous anger with your friend. Talk about why you are angry. Did you read an upsetting news article or see a hurtful video? Did you experience or witness racism firsthand? What happened? Talk about how the experience made you feel and whether it reminded you of prior experiences. Particularly if you are a person of color, this can feel risky because you may not know how the other person is going to respond. You may also not be mentally or emotionally prepared to discuss this topic with someone who you think won't understand the reasons for your anger. Whether it is now or later, a true cross-racial friendship will require some amount of openness and vulnerability. You will have to bring your whole self to the table, righteous anger and all.

A commitment to openness by sharing righteous anger should be met with a complementary commitment to listen without judgment. If we respond to our friend's expression of righteous anger with defensiveness, anger, or deflection, we signal that some topics are off-limits. We may say that we want to enter into a cross-racial friendship, but only if

> *A true cross-racial friendship will require some amount of openness and vulnerability. You will have to bring your whole self to the table, righteous anger and all.*

we don't talk about things like mass incarceration or the continued segregation of public education. When we don't hold to a commitment to listen to righteous anger without judgment, the kudzu takes over and forms a wall between us. Defensiveness and deflection say, "I don't want to build a friendship with the real you. I want to build a friendship with your proxy." We have to get over the sense that there are aspects of race or racism that are off-limits in cross-racial relationships. Our comfort is not worth the silencing of our friends. A commitment to openness by sharing righteous anger and to listening without judgment is foundational for authentic cross-racial friendships. Not only is it foundational, it's also where the transformation happens. Embrace righteous anger and you may find that, in both the telling and the listening, love and empathy take root. Perhaps you can begin to share in the righteous anger, and then who knows how God might use you to disrupt systemic racism together.

But there is also another kind of anger—the kind that the saints of the church named a deadly sin. That kind of anger is not a healthy or helpful response to injustice. It is, rather, selfish, defensive, and embittering. This anger can be manipulative or even hostile. We've all felt it, every one of us—about a million things, not just about race. We've all been angry when someone cuts us off in traffic, when our meal takes too long to arrive at a restaurant, and when we find ourselves waiting in long lines. The world is full of things large and small to make us angry. But unrighteous anger when it comes to race is particularly sinister because of its potential to destroy relationships.

When it comes to race, we tend to use this second kind of anger as a tool of evasion. In conversations about race, most of us experience some discomfort. Often, the response to these first signs of discomfort is anger and defensiveness. The goal becomes to avoid having the conversation at all. We use anger to deflect and distract from the task of having these hard conversations. The state of having a low tolerance for discomfort in conversations about race has been called "white fragility."[2] Anger at the first sign of a conversation about race indicates that white fragility is at play.

While we can lean into righteous anger as a possible

> *The state of having a low tolerance for discomfort in conversations about race has been called "white fragility." Anger at the first sign of a conversation about race indicates that white fragility is at play.*

path to deeper friendship, anger that is rooted in bitterness, fragility, defensiveness, or other deflective postures will derail the friendship and must be rooted out. You might use two strategies for tackling this unwanted, unhelpful, and unholy anger: decenter yourself, and lean into the reconciling and transforming power of the Holy Spirit.

The story of a pastor friend is helpful in illustrating the first strategy—decentering yourself. As she was considering ordination, our friend had concerns about the status of women's ordination in her denomination. Although her local church was willing to ordain her, she knew that some churches in her denomination would not consider ordaining a woman. Hoping for some guidance, she went to speak to another woman pastor in her denomination. Should she seek ordination in a denomination where the matter of ordination of women was not settled in all churches? The pastor's response was a bit shocking. She matter-of-factly said, "This is not about you. This is about a call to come and die." The pastor was asking our friend to decenter herself in the process of discerning her own call to be a pastor, because this was about something larger and more important than she. In the same way, when anger arises in the process of building cross-racial friendships, decenter yourself. Remember that this is not about defending a position, whether you're white or black. This is about something much greater. This is about reaching across racial and cultural divides to form friendships that could impact both the individuals involved and the kingdom of God by laying the groundwork for disrupting racism. Anger is likely to arise in these friendships, but if we can decenter ourselves, we may find there is more room for friendship to flourish.

The second strategy in dealing with anger is to lean into the power of the Holy Spirit. The Holy Spirit is a reconciling power. The Book of Acts recounts the coming of the Holy Spirit on the day of Pentecost. Following Jesus's death, burial, and resurrection, He ascended into heaven (Acts 1:6-11). Just as Jesus predicted, the Holy Spirit enveloped the disciples (Acts 1:8, 2:1-4).

It may be worth pausing here for a minute to understand the magnitude of this event. The disciples had watched Jesus Christ crucified on a Roman cross like a common criminal. They thought the story of Jesus was at an end. None were waiting at the tomb for Jesus to rise again, but He did. Then Jesus told them to wait. They were to wait in Jerusalem until they had been "clothed with power from on high" (Luke 24:49). Then Jesus was gone, carried up into heaven (Luke 24:51). This must have been confusing. Jesus returns only to leave again, and His instruction is just to wait? But they waited anyway.

Luke picks up this account of the day of Pentecost in the Book of Acts, where he writes that "suddenly from heaven there came a sound like the rush of a violent wind" (Acts 2:2 NRSV). It was the Holy Spirit. It came suddenly. It came loudly. It came in power. And it filled the entire house. Jesus had ascended into heaven, but the Holy Spirit had arrived. The first evidence that the disciples were filled with the Holy Spirit was that they were able to speak in the languages of various nations and tribes, though they were all Galileans (Acts 2:4-11). The Holy Spirit removed the barriers of language and ethnicity so that all could hear of God's power. This same boundary-busting Spirit is in you. All who profess Jesus Christ as Lord have received the Holy Spirit, which dwells in them. The reconciling power of the Holy Spirit is powerful enough to counter your anger, helping you transcend racial and ethnic barriers. You need only lean into and rely on the Spirit's power.

Not only is the Holy Spirit a reconciling power; it is also a transforming power that prepares us for the task of deep cross-racial relationships. If you are a Christian, you have two choices: live by the

Holy Spirit or live by the desires of the flesh. The apostle Paul sets up this dichotomy in Galatians 5. According to Paul, what the Holy Spirit desires is opposed to the works of the flesh (Galatians 5:17-18). Paul is clear about what behaviors are among these Spirit-opposing works of the flesh. Anger, strife, and quarrels are among them (Galatians 5:20). In contrast to the works of the flesh, the Holy Spirit causes a different set of qualities to manifest in us: "The fruit of the Spirit is love, joy, peace, patience, kindness, generosity, faithfulness, gentleness, and self-control" (Galatians 5:22-23).

Imagine how our interactions with those who are different from us would deepen if they were characterized by love and peace rather than anger, joy and patience rather than strife, or patience and kindness rather than a quarrelsome spirit. The transforming power of the Holy Spirit, the power to manifest the fruit of the Spirit, is in you. God

> *We can be so transformed that we desire God's justice more than being right, more than maintaining power, more than our comfort, perhaps more than anything.*

desires for us to embody these qualities not so that we seem like good people. Mere personal piety is not the goal of the Christian faith. God desires for us to be transformed by the power of the Holy Spirit so that we might engage with God in the reconciling and transforming work that God is already doing. We can be so transformed that we desire God's justice more than being right, more than maintaining power, more than our comfort, perhaps more than anything. It means listening when you would rather talk, staying when you would rather leave, and leaning in when you would rather be closed off. It means showing love even when you are angry.

DISCUSSION QUESTIONS

1. Regardless of your race, what tends to provoke your anger when it comes to racial issues? Why does that particular thing make you angry?

2. How do you tell the difference between righteous and unrighteous anger?

3. Have you ever experienced "white fragility"? What impact did it have on your conversation?

4. Do you think there is a difference between feeling fragile and actually being fragile? Discuss why or why not. How do you go about being less fragile?

5. Why is the fruit of the Spirit (see Galatians 5:22-23) so important when it comes to having conversations about race and racism?

Chapter Nine

WHAT HOLDS RACISM IN PLACE?

The devil does not sleep, nor is the flesh yet dead; therefore, you must never cease your preparation for battle, because on the right and on the left are enemies who never rest.

—*Thomas à Kempis*

During World War II, C. S. Lewis was asked by the BBC to give a series of radio broadcasts for the city of London. The war was not going well for England. London was being bombed regularly by Nazi Germany. Civilians were dying by the thousands. The BBC asked Lewis to talk about Christianity in the hope that the city would be encouraged.

The ensuing series of talks offered a masterful overview of the Christian faith. They were collected in printed form and eventually published as a book titled *Mere Christianity*. Seventy years later, it is still in print. Millions of people have read it. It is considered one of the most influential books on Christianity ever published.

In his lecture titled "The Invasion," Lewis came to the topic of pain: What did Christianity have to say about why there was so much pain and suffering in the world? Lewis suggested that there was an evil power at work. This evil power, he explained, was created by God but had rebelled against God's authority. It became the source of the death, disease, and sin that has plagued humanity since the beginning of time. Lewis anticipated that some of his audience would object to such an idea. Attempting to give voice to their skepticism, he said, "Do you really mean, at this time of day, to re-introduce our old friend the devil . . . ?" He then replied, "Yes I do."[1]

We want to do the same thing. Most people think humans sustain racism. But we think there are more than humans involved. It seems to us that if you discount this aspect of the struggle, you place yourself at a significant disadvantage. To rule out the involvement of what the apostle Paul refers to as "principalities and powers" will leave us tactically vulnerable. It would be like bringing a spray bottle to a house fire. The intentions are good, but the strategy for solving the problem is tragically underpowered.

Lewis, it's worth noting, wrote a letter in February 1955, mentioning that belief in this being called Satan is not essential to being a Christian.[2] In a similar fashion, we realize that believing in Satan is not essential to working against racism. So, feel free to skip this chapter. But before you do, you might want to consider the fanciful advice Lewis's friend, J. R. R. Tolkien, once offered, "It does not do to leave a live dragon out of your calculations if you live near him."[3]

So, we begin by noting, as previously mentioned, that the apostle Paul takes recourse to this idea of an evil power in attempting to make sense of his own reality. He was writing a letter from a Roman prison (he'd been incarcerated for advocating what was then considered to be a minor, quirky Jewish sect) to a church in the ancient city of Ephesus.

Writing from prison, there is little doubt that occasionally Paul must have reflected on the course his life had taken. He had gone from being the powerful, internationally known defender of Judaism to a powerless prisoner. As he reflected on this turn of events, he wrote, "For we are not contending against flesh and blood, but against the principalities, against the powers, against the world rulers of this present darkness, against the spiritual hosts of wickedness in the heavenly places" (Ephesians 6:12).

It's important to think carefully about this. What are these principalities, powers, and world rulers? What's their agenda? How do they operate? To what extent are they involved in human affairs, and more specifically, to what degree are they involved with racism? If we discover they are involved, then what exactly are we supposed to do about it?

Regarding this last question, if we don't think principalities and powers are involved, we'll do nothing about them. If we think "powers" is just a rhetorical holdover from an archaic age that believed in all sorts of fairy tales and superstitions that have been debunked by modern science, then they are free to pursue their agenda unopposed. It's like a hacker who gets into your computer files undetected. If you don't know the hacker's there, she can do whatever she wants with no interference from you—a hacker's dream come true!

So, it comes as no surprise that the first order of business for these mysterious suprahuman forces is to convince you that they don't exist. This is exactly what they have done. They have deployed a stealth strategy that is extremely effective. If you took logic and rhetoric in high school or college, you've heard of this strategy before. Granted, your teacher probably didn't mention it in this particular context, but he or she no doubt took some time to make sure you understood something called the straw man argument. It's a brilliantly simple tactic for persuading people to conclude that something should be disregarded. It goes like this: if you want people to disbelieve or discredit a certain thing, whether it's a political point of view or, in our case, principalities or powers, create a caricature of the thing you want people to discount. It should be something so silly that no intelligent person would believe it.

Next (and here's where the sleight of hand comes in), make sure that whenever the topic comes up, people are thinking about the silly caricature, not the reality behind the caricature. They will dismiss the caricature because it's absurd. In doing so, they will think they've made an intelligent decision about the real thing, but they never thought about the real thing. They only thought about the caricature, or as the science of rhetoric calls it, the straw man.

So, let me ask you a question. When you hear the word *devil*, what image comes to mind? If it's some sort of bright red creature with a tail, horns, and pitchfork, then perhaps you are thinking about a straw man. Perhaps the reality behind the caricature is something you've never seriously considered. For the rest of this chapter, we will attempt to focus on that reality.

Here is the issue before us. If these principalities and powers aren't humanoid figures running around with pitchforks, then what are they? In addition to the helpful thinking provided by C. S. Lewis, another Englishman added some clarity to the issue. Lesslie Newbigin was a missiologist and theologian who studied at Cambridge University. He went on to serve as a missionary in India from 1936 until 1974, when he returned to England. He published essential books on the interface between the gospel and culture. In *The Gospel in a Pluralist Society*, he devotes a whole chapter to grappling with the idea of principalities and powers. Therein, he makes space for intelligent, thoughtful Christians to explore the role that principalities and powers play in the world

Rather than summarizing Newbigin's work, we'd like to show you what Newbigin's ideas reveal when they are put alongside the life story of one man. The man's name is Bull Connor.

Theophilus Eugene Connor was born on July 11, 1897, in Selma, Alabama. He grew up and acquired no small amount of political ambition. As a result, for more than twenty years he served as the elected commissioner of public safety for the city of Birmingham. He was in that role during the height of the civil rights movement in the early 1960s.

It was Bull Connor who arrested Martin Luther King Jr. on April 12, 1963, thereby enabling Dr. King to write his famous "Letter from a Birmingham Jail." It was Bull Connor who was responsible for some of the most disturbing images of the civil rights movement. You've seen the black-and-white photos of fire hoses being turned on black children? Bull Connor gave that order. You've seen the pictures of a police dog tearing the shirt off a black protester? Bull Connor was the man who ordered the police to turn those dogs loose. At one point, Bull Connor gave a directive to the Birmingham Police Department that ultimately jailed more than ten thousand people engaged in the civil rights movement.[4]

As we reflect on Connor's activities, several questions come to mind: What motivated him to cause so much fear and suffering? Was it hate? Was he himself afraid? If so, where did that fear come from? What was Connor trying to protect? Clearly, he had an image of the way things ought to be. Where did those images come from? And finally, Bull Connor acted with impunity based on the authority given him by the city of Birmingham, which in turn was sanctioned by the state of Alabama. Where did that power come from, and how did it turn into a force that clearly worked against the human freedom it was supposedly created to protect?

Lesslie Newbigin's theories help us understand Bull Connor. In the following passage, Newbigin is referring to Herod and Pontius Pilate, historical figures familiar to readers of the Gospels. Like Bull Connor, Herod and Pontius Pilate were government officials who figured prominently in a tragic miscarriage of justice. The connection with our story here is unmissable. Newbigin says:

> Are we talking about an individual called Herod or Pilate or Smith or Jones, or are we talking about something which is temporarily embodied in these office-holders? . . . And when (according to the Fourth Gospel) Jesus speaks of his coming death and says "Now is the judgment of this world, now shall the ruler of this world be cast out" (John 12:31) he cannot be speaking just of Herod or Pilate; neither of them could be called ruler of this world.[5]

So, what exactly is Newbigin talking about?

> Clearly this language does not simply refer to certain human beings who hold these offices of power and authority for a few years and are then dead and gone. They refer to something behind these individuals, to the offices, the powers, the authority which is represented from time to time by this or that individual. It is these powers, authorities, rulers, dominions which have been confronted in Christ's death with the supreme power and authority of God.[6]

Bull Connor, like Herod and Pilate before him, was not just an agent for a local municipality. He was a means through which something much bigger than that acted. This something is identified by Jesus when he talks about "the ruler of this world." This something is named by the apostle Paul when he points out that we are not struggling against flesh and blood but against "principalities and powers."

These powers used Herod and Pilate. They also used Bull Connor. Ultimately, those who seek to destroy what is good, whether in 1963 or AD 33, have been deceived, empowered, and deployed by the same mysterious force. Sometimes that force shows up in human affairs in the form of a snake. Sometimes it shows up as a dictator or a king. Sometimes it shows up as the commissioner of public safety. How can we tell? Jesus says we will know them by their fruits (Matthew 7:16). So when you smell the rotten fruit of hatred, of hubris, of dehumanization, of destruction and injustice, know that these mysterious forces are present and on the move. Newbigin says, "Simply to ignore [them] as some sort of outdated mythology would be a disastrous mistake."[7]

So, when we talk about the devil, we don't mean the red-horned pitchfork-carrier. We mean, with Newbigin, that

> the principalities and powers are realities. We may
> not be able to visualize them, to locate them, or to say
> exactly what they are. But we are foolish if we pretend
> that they do not exist. Certainly one cannot read the
> Gospels without recognizing that the ministry of Jesus
> from beginning to end was a mighty spiritual battle
> with powers which are not simply human frailties,
> errors, diseases, or sins.[8]

Now that we've attributed the pain and suffering Bull Connor inflicted on so many people to the influence of these principalities and powers, we need to be clear on what we are not saying. We are not suggesting Bull Connor was demon-possessed. We are not suggesting that he not be held responsible for his actions. Neither are we suggesting that he was some sort of Satanist. Like you and me, Bull Connor was a complex mixture of the image of God and the corruption of that image. To fail to extend that recognition to him is to become guilty of dehumanizing him in the same way he dehumanized black people.

Our contention here is that Bull Connor was the unwitting dupe of forces that he likely didn't know existed. Our enemy is referred to as the father of lies (John 8:44). He can appear as an angel of light (2 Corinthians 11:14). We can all be deceived. In Bull Connor's case, however, the toxic mixture of fear and his thirst for political power in the midst of social chaos created a perfect storm. It made him particularly susceptible to being used as a tool of evil. As a result, thousands of people suffered. Many died. But we can't waste time hating Bull Connor. Instead, we must let him serve as a warning. There are Bull Connors and Herods alive today. There are Hitlers and Pilates and Stalins loose in the world right now who are in the midst of their own perfect storms. In light of that, we have to ask: What are we supposed to do?

Four imperatives in the New Testament provide us with some practical advice. The first is to be prepared: when you push against evil, be prepared for evil to push back. In light of this, Jesus tells us to count the cost (Luke 14:28). If principalities and powers are involved in sustaining racism, then we need to be prepared for a long, hard battle. A speech here and a rally there are valuable. And, of course, creating friendships with people who don't look like you is foundational. But to think these things will make the problem vanish in a couple of months or even a couple of years is to misunderstand the nature of the opposition. The battle against racism was going on before we were born. It will continue after we die. This calls for perseverance, but we can persevere with a great deal of hope.

Indeed, the second New Testament imperative is to be hopeful. The kingdom of God is not in trouble. Never has been. Never will be. It will ultimately win this battle. That outcome has been secured by Christ's death and resurrection. Considering that world-changing reality, Paul says, "I consider that the sufferings of this present time are not worth comparing with the glory that is to be revealed to us" (Romans 8:18). So know this: there is not one kind word you'll utter, not one evil-defying act you'll perform, not one stand against dehumanization that is wasted. Everything you say, everything you do is being leveraged by God to bring about the end of suffering. We do not labor in vain. God's got this. Count on it. The best is yet to come.

> *There is not one kind word you'll utter, not one evil-defying act you'll perform, not one stand against dehumanization that is wasted. Everything you say, everything you do is being leveraged by God to bring about the end of suffering.*

The third imperative is to be alert. The principalities and powers are on the move. We must pay attention. This is one of the more common imperatives in the New Testament, occurring more than twenty times in various places. In 1 John 4:1, we are told to "test the spirits to see whether they are of God." In 1 Peter 5:8, it says, "Be sober. Be watchful. Your adversary the devil prowls around like a roaring lion, seeking some one to devour."

The twenty-first-century version of this idea is to be fully present. Don't miss what is in front of you. There are opportunities everywhere. There are also threats and lies. Being alert, being fully present, positions us to catch these and act appropriately. A person who lives fully present will find there is not enough time in the day to take advantage of all the opportunities before her. The person who is alert is never bored, never without a sense of purpose, never lacking opportunity to love people. Being alert is the catalyst that can activate the ideas you'll encounter in this book. We will not make a difference if we do not first make ourselves alert.

The last imperative is the most important one and, perhaps, the one we are most tempted to skip. If principalities and powers are involved in racism, then we must pray. To neglect prayer in the face of such an enemy is to allow our hubris to rob us of that which will best protect us and propel us forward. We will go further and faster in our efforts to disrupt racism if we pray.

Don't take our word for it. Read your history books. Who was at the center of the civil rights movement in the 1960s? Christians who understood the power of prayer. Who was a key figure in the dismantling of apartheid in South Africa? Nobel Peace Prize winner Desmond Tutu, the archbishop of Cape Town. His book *No Future Without Forgiveness* is laced throughout with references to prayer. Who led the nineteenth-century movement to outlaw slavery in England? It was William Wilberforce, who said, "Of all things, guard against neglecting God in the secret place of prayer." And a hundred years from now, if the world lasts, who will be the people who made the greatest inroads against racism in the twenty-first century? The people who prayed against this great evil. You and I can be those people. And as you'll see in the next chapter, we're going to need all the prayer we can get.

DISCUSSION QUESTIONS

1. Is the idea that principalities and powers are involved in sustaining racism a new idea for you? Does the idea that some sort of supra-human evil power is involved in racism sound plausible to you? Why or why not?

2. Have you ever encountered any form of evil that you knew at the time had some sort of connection with a supernatural evil power? If so, please describe your experience.

3. In this chapter, Bull Connor, the commissioner of public safety in Birmingham, Alabama, during the civil rights movement, is compared to the biblical figures of Herod and Pontius Pilate. How do you feel about that comparison?

4. Because suprahuman evil powers are involved in the affairs of human beings, Teesha and John suggest four practical responses to this reality. What are they? Which one is easiest for you? Which one is the most difficult?

5. Why do you think so many of the key figures in the fight against racism were Christians? Do you think Christians are leading the fight against racism today? Do you think they should be? Why or why not?

Chapter Ten

FESS UP

The past, far from disappearing or lying down and being quiet, has an embarrassing and persistent way of returning and haunting us unless it has in fact been dealt with adequately.

—Desmond Tutu, *No Future Without Forgiveness*

Get over it." This is what some white people, some Christian white people, have to say to black people who are still carrying the pain, frustration, and anger of encountering racism. What is contained in those three small words? To begin, "get over it" implies that racism is a thing of the past. As we pointed out in chapter 1, this is not true. Acts of racism continue to occur every day in the United States. It's hard to get over something when that something is not over. When you tell someone to get over something that's still happening, what you're really saying is "get used to it."

Second, "get over it" implies that the pain of racism is not the white speaker's problem. It implies that there is nothing for white people to do except watch and wait (perhaps impatiently) while black people struggle with their pain and anger. It will be worth our while to take a minute and look at a couple of biblical texts that speak to this idea. Together, they make it crystal clear that there is more for white people to do, especially Christian white people, than stand around waiting for their black brothers and sisters to figure out what to do with four hundred years of racial injustice.

The Sermon on the Mount is perhaps Jesus's most famous body of teaching. Early on in the sermon, Jesus says, "So if you are offering your gift at the altar, and there remember that your brother has something against you, leave your gift there before the altar and go; first be reconciled to your brother, and then come and offer your gift" (Matthew 5:23-24).

> *"Get over it" implies that the pain of racism is not the white speaker's problem. It implies that there is nothing for white people to do except watch and wait.*

In this text, Jesus places a great deal of emphasis on *reconciliation*. Jesus refers to the Jewish practice of bringing a gift—in other words, a sacrifice—to the altar of the Jewish temple. In the first century, this practice was at the center of Jewish religious life. Thousands of priests assisted the entire Jewish nation in presenting their sacrificial gifts to God at the altar. This was how the Jewish people received God's grace and forgiveness. To fail to do this was to stand outside of the provision God made for the Jewish people to atone for their sin. As incredible as it must have seemed to the thousands of individuals who stood in line every day to offer their gift to God, Jesus says, "Hold up. There is something I want you to do BEFORE you offer your gift." In other words, Jesus is saying that being reconciled to your brother or sister is of the highest priority, so much so that it ought to interrupt the process of bringing your sacrifices to God. In other words, Jesus suggests that before you turn to God for peace, make peace with your brother.

Jesus doesn't place any limits on what should be included here. Pretty much anything that has given offense to your brother is on the table. And racism has certainly caused black brothers and sisters a great deal of offense. As such, pursuing racial reconciliation becomes a priority not because a civil rights activist says so. Not because a "progressive" theologian says so. Not because celebrities are tweeting about racial issues. Reconciliation is a priority because Jesus says so.

> *Pursuing racial reconciliation becomes a priority not because a civil rights activist says so. Not because a "progressive" theologian says so. Not because celebrities are tweeting about racial issues. Reconciliation is a priority because Jesus says so.*

As we reflect on this, there's a very important nuance to catch. It has to do with what should trigger the disruption of our worship life. It's not that we have something against somebody. It's that somebody has something against us. In other words, it's not our pain that should trigger a disruption. It's the pain that we've caused someone else. We may or may not feel like that pain is valid. But it's not our point of view that

Jesus cites as the reason for leaving our gift at the altar. It's the fact that a brother or sister is in pain and that they attribute that pain to us.

It is doubtful that telling them to "get over it" aligns with what Jesus had in mind here. The fact is that reconciliation asks more of us than simply telling people what to do with their pain. Upon hearing this, people in the "get over it" camp often respond by saying, "Well, what do you want me to do? I can't go around apologizing to millions of black people! And who is this 'brother' that Jesus talks about anyway? I'm not even sure who that is." Interestingly enough, somebody asked Jesus a similar question two thousand years ago.

We're referring to a conversation between Jesus and a lawyer that is captured in Luke 10: 25-37. They were talking about loving God and loving your neighbor. In the course of the conversation, the lawyer asked Jesus, "And who is my neighbor?" For our purposes here, we will assume that the word *neighbor* in Luke 10 is synonymous with the word *brother* in Matthew 5.

The text says that the lawyer asked the question in an attempt to justify himself. The phrase "justify himself" is important. It alludes to the fact that the lawyer experienced some dissonance when he heard Jesus talk about loving your neighbor. He felt an uncomfortable gap between where he was and where Jesus wanted him to be. Jesus was asking him to enlarge his understanding of "neighbor." The lawyer was operating with a very narrow definition of "neighbor." He likely understood "neighbor" to refer exclusively to people who looked, spoke, and believed like he did—in other words, his fellow Jews. Jesus had a much more generous idea in mind. The lawyer clearly wanted to eliminate this dissonance by, in effect, asking Jesus to shrink the idea of "neighbor" to a size he felt comfortable with. Jesus did exactly the opposite. He proceeded to tell the parable of the Good Samaritan.

If you're not familiar with the parable of the Good Samaritan, now would be a great time to read it. Briefly put, it's a story about a Samaritan (that is, a member of a group of people with whom the Jews had deep tension and enmity) who stopped to help a man (probably a Jew) whom he found in a ditch, the victim of robbers who beat him up, took his stuff, and left him for dead. It is of special significance in the story that the Samaritan found the wounded man after two Jewish spiritual leaders had walked right by him.

As is the case with all the stories Jesus told, we could talk about this one for hours. But for now, we want to point out just one thing. The Samaritan wasn't to blame for the suffering the man in the ditch endured. He wasn't even around when the robbery happened. But he helped him anyway. He helped not because he was culpable but because he was connected. He saw the man in the ditch as his neighbor. This answers our question. Our neighbor is the suffering person in front of us. We may or may not be complicit in their suffering, but their suffering is our business because they are our neighbor.

Let's take a minute to knit together Matthew 5:23-24 and Luke 10:25-37. Briefly put, Jesus is asking us to see suffering people as our neighbors, especially if we are responsible for their suffering. And as such, these suffering neighbors are not distractions; they are priorities—so much so that Jesus asks us to disrupt our lives, whether in church or on the road, for their sake. And in the space that disruption creates, we are to do two things: pursue reconciliation and provide assistance. We'll talk a bit more about what that assistance looks like in chapter 17. For the rest of this chapter, we want to focus on the idea of reconciliation.

"Get over it" will never produce reconciliation; but if we ask, "How can I help you get over it?" a process is launched. With a little care and a lot of prayer, this process can produce the reconciliation Jesus instructed us to pursue. There must be a thousand ways to pursue reconciliation. We'd like to talk about a very simple approach. It consists of three parts: lament, repent, and prevent.

We will talk about the idea of lamenting more in chapter 12. For now, we want to define it simply as the articulation of hurt and anger.[1] Or, to give that an explicitly Christian gloss, it is the articulation *before God* of hurt and anger. The first step in pursuing racial reconciliation is to join in lament with our black brothers and sisters. There is four hundred years' worth of injustice, slavery, and abuse on the table here to be worked through, not to mention what happened today and what will happen tomorrow. When a white person can own a sense of holy discomfort and join with black people in articulating their hurt and anger, a huge gap between the races is breached. We become one voice before God, lamenting the horrible treatment of black people.

> *"Get over it" will never produce reconciliation; but if we ask, "How can I help you get over it?" a process is launched.*

Of course, lamenting four hundred years' worth of pain can be a daunting task, so we have a suggestion. Rather than attempting to lament four hundred years of history, how about starting with what you encounter in the life of one black friend? If you don't have any black friends, then skip ahead to chapter 17, "Friendship 101." Then come back and finish this chapter.

Before we move on, there's one other thing to consider. In the spirit of the Good Samaritan, who was not responsible for the suffering of the man in the ditch, the opportunity to lament is before us whether we are complicit in the suffering or not. We can lament even if we are not to blame. Lamenting sin is not the same thing as confessing sin. But before we pronounce ourselves innocent, we need to do a little soul searching.

The very first thing Jesus said when He began His public ministry was, "'Repent, for the kingdom of heaven is at hand'" (Matthew 4:17). Scholars tell us that the best definition of the word *repent* is "to change your mind."[2] So Jesus is essentially saying, "Okay! Now that I'm here, it's important to start thinking differently about things. I'm doing something new in the world, and the old ways of thinking will no longer work very well." In other words, because Jesus's coming has changed the world, our thinking must change.

> *When a white person can own a sense of holy discomfort and join with black people in articulating their hurt and anger, a huge gap between the races is breached.*

Other New Testament authors add their voice to what Jesus said, reminding us that thinking differently is always followed by acting differently (see James 2:14-17). So here's the task before us: in light of the fact that the kingdom of heaven is now here, do we need to change the way we think and act when it comes to issues of racial justice? There is a time to think about this at a national level. There is a time to think about this in terms of our state and our city. But asking questions about repentance must always begin at a very personal level. Do you and I need to think and act differently?

We mustn't rush to judgment here. The best answers to this question will come after we've engaged in some self-examination, or what is popularly referred to as a "gut check." And that will take some courage, because the things we might find buried inside us may not be very pleasant. Bigotry? racial pride? resentment? hatred? smugness? a voracious thirst for power? The list goes on and on. These are all common. They may or may not be hiding in your soul. That said, there is one sin that is fairly common, particularly among white people. It's the sin of apathy. Bernice King, Martin Luther King Jr.'s daughter, says that hatred didn't kill her father. She says it was apathy. Martin Luther King Jr. himself put it this way: "History will have to record that the greatest tragedy of this period of social transition was not the strident clamor of the bad people, but the appalling silence of the good people."[3]

How do we repent of apathy? Doing so is both simple and challenging: find somebody to whom you can confess your sin. Then find somebody to care about. We can't repent of the sin of apathy in isolation from the people we have failed to care about. And we are commanded to confess our sins to one another (see James 5:16). If confessing to God alone were enough, Jesus would not have commanded us in Matthew 5 to leave our gift at the altar.

When we find a friend who doesn't look like us, we will also find someone to whom we can confess our apathy. We will find someone to care about who looks unlike anyone we've cared about before. That said, this calls for wisdom. There is such a thing as moving too far too fast. The friendship must be allowed to grow strong enough to bear the weight of such a confession. This doesn't happen overnight, but it can happen. Every time it does, the kingdom of heaven takes a small step forward, reclaiming territory that had previously been captured by the enemy.

The final part of helping people "get over it" is prevention. Once we "weep with those who weep" (lament) and confess our sin (repent) we are ready to move out together to work against the racism that has caused so much pain in the world (prevention.)

Shortly after Jesus talks about leaving our gifts at the altar, He talks about being salt and light (see Matthew 5:13-16). When we befriend people who don't look like us, we encounter vast possibilities, far beyond the capacity of any book to catalogue, for being salt and light in the world. The fact that such friendships even exist is itself a powerful witness to the reconciling power of Jesus Christ. Beyond that, the sky's the limit. Letting God reshape how we think, how we see the institutions that shape our culture, how we pray, how we vote, who we spend time with, how we spend our money, how we speak, and how we live (personally and corporately) are all on the table.

Some church people say this distracts us from evangelism and discipleship. On the contrary, working to prevent racism gives credibility to the gospel. It adds a new, practical dimension to our discipleship. It makes a way for the love of Jesus Christ to flow into a world that seems to be trending toward polarization and tribalism. Lament, repent, and prevent? Heck. That doesn't distract people from Jesus. It points people toward Him. And there's never been a time in the world when that's more needed than right now.

> *Some church people say this distracts us from evangelism and discipleship. On the contrary, working to prevent racism gives credibility to the gospel.*

DISCUSSION QUESTIONS

1. Has anyone ever told you to "get over" something? How did that feel to you? Was it a justified request or did it feel unfair? Was it helpful? Did it serve as a motivation to work through whatever the issue was?

2. In Matthew 5, Jesus says to be reconciled to your brother before you offer your gift at the altar. As Teesha and John explained, Jesus was referring to the temple sacrifices in which the whole Jewish nation participated. What does this look like when it's applied to twenty-first-century Christianity as it's practiced in the United States?

3. In the discussion about the parable of the Good Samaritan, John and Teesha explain why the Samaritan helped the man in the ditch. They said, "He helped not because he was culpable but because he was connected." What does this mean?

4. This chapter suggests that one way to pursue reconciliation is to "lament, repent, and prevent." Do you think this is a useful way to practice reconciliation? Why or why not?

5. Teesha and John point out that repenting from sin involves confessing sin. Furthermore, they suggest that confessing your sins should involve confessing them not only to God but also to another human being. Do you agree?

6. Some Christians feel that working for racial reconciliation/justice is a distraction from evangelism and discipleship. John and Teesha disagree. What do you think?

Chapter Eleven

SPECKS AND PLANKS

My guiding principle is this: guilt is never to be doubted.

—Franz Kafka

Dissonance. It's a specific kind of tension, a clashing of perspectives that sets us on edge. It's like choosing to wear your pajamas to a black-tie dinner party. There is a conflict between what you are expected to wear and what you choose to wear. That clash between expectation and behavior creates dissonance, and dissonance begs to be resolved. If you show up in your pajamas at a black-tie dinner party, you will quickly be asked to either leave or change your clothes. Additionally, avoiding dissonance is a powerful motivation among us humans. So, you will likely never be invited to another black-tie dinner party. Just something to keep in mind . . .

There are other kinds of dissonance. Sometimes mystery writers use dissonance as a literary device that will keep us turning the page because we want to arrive at the resolution of the plot. Composers will sometimes create a musical dissonance in the second-to-the-last chord of a symphony in order to give that final chord, which resolves the dissonance, a great deal of power.

There's also dissonance within the ethical realm of human behavior. It's that uncomfortable, almost unbearable, feeling we get when we violate our moral compass. You and I might disagree about what's right and wrong, but we both have the same experience when we break our respective rules. It's a sense of dissonance, a painful recognition of the gap between what we feel is right and what we actually did. We have a name for this moral dissonance. It's called guilt.

Most people will go to extraordinary lengths to avoid feeling guilty. We'll stay busy so we don't have to think about it. We'll self-medicate to try and make the pain of guilt go away. Sometimes we'll earnestly explain to others or ourselves why we weren't really to blame for what we did.

Jesus mentions another favorite tactic of ours that we employ when trying to resolve moral dissonance. When confronted with our own guilt, we will sometimes attempt to identify the moral failing of someone else and suggest that their moral infraction is worse than ours, thereby creating the illusion that our guilt is diminished. He uses the metaphor of specks and logs in people's eyes to make the point, or as the New International Version of the Bible puts it, specks and planks.

Jesus, with that unerring insight of His into human behavior, calls us out here. He takes our "little speck in my eye is nothing compared to the plank in my brother's eye" tactic and reverses it. In Matthew 7:3, He says, "'Why do you look at the speck of sawdust in your brother's eye and pay no attention to the plank in your own eye?'" He defeats our attempt to avoid culpability because now the plank is in my eye, not in the eye of my brother or sister. By the way, Jesus is not trying to create a hierarchy of sin. Rather, He is referencing the all-too-human tendency to maximize the sin of our brother or sister in the hope that it will minimize our sin. If I can make your sin look bigger, it will hopefully make my sin look smaller.

The truth is that the speck and plank game doesn't really work. When I'm being honest with myself, I know that whatever it is that you did doesn't really affect my moral status. Morality isn't graded on a curve. And, of course, that's why we often refuse to be honest with ourselves. If my only strategy for diminishing my guilt is to focus on other people's guilt, then honesty will bring my sense of guilt crashing back into my mind.

There's a sense of tragedy in all this. For starters, it's all unnecessary. God's grace makes specks and planks a waste of time. Using them to get out from under our guilt when God's grace is available is like paddling a boat with a spoon when there's a five-hundred-horsepower engine available. The spoon doesn't really work. It's exhausting to try, and you stay in the same place. Furthermore, when I

> *When I'm being honest with myself, I know that whatever it is that you did doesn't really affect my moral status. Morality isn't graded on a curve.*

attempt to use your sin to diminish my sin, our relationship becomes adversarial. At that point I'm trying to throw you under the bus. Friends don't throw friends under the bus.

Sadly, a lot of church people are still in the speck and plank business. And some of those church people employ this strategy when it comes to talking about racism. Let us show you what we mean. The following is the synthesis of several conversations John has had in the past year. We've switched around the details so nobody will feel like we've thrown them under the bus.

Not too long ago, John was meeting in his office with a friend of mine who happens to be white. She's a great person—a good wife, a kind and loving mother, and a vital part of several ministries at our church. She knew John was an author and asked about what he was currently writing. John told her about the book that you are holding in your hand or listening to right now. The minute she knew what he was writing about, there was a slight change in the atmosphere of their conversation. A tiny rift appeared. Nothing huge. Almost imperceptible. A moment before, they had been together. Suddenly, they were not quite on the same page.

She said, "Can I ask you a question?"

"Sure!" John replied.

"What about all the black-on-black crime? And what about the absence of a father figure in so many black families?"

Boom.

There it was. She had just pointed out what she thought was a plank in her fellow human being's eye.

Here's another example. A couple of years ago, on Martin Luther King Jr.'s birthday, another upstanding, white, church-going person wrote a blog post that he sent to me. In it, he wondered aloud what Martin Luther King Jr. would think about the current state of "his" culture today, referring, of course, to the black community. The blogger then proceeded to (you guessed it) offer a moral critique of the black community. His tone may have been respectful, but his content was insulting. There was no celebration of MLK's courage. There was no sorrow expressed for the great evil that made Dr. King's sacrifice necessary. There was only a condescending description of what he considered to be a log in the eye of the black community.

We could go on. We've had these conversations in the South. We've also had them in Southern California. These people are decent human beings. In some ways, they are much better people than we are. We don't think they hate black people. But when someone is so quick to point out somebody else's shortcomings, that tells us something. Only people who are experiencing some kind of moral dissonance, some kind of guilt, engage in this type of behavior. The only people who play the speck and plank game are those who have something in their eye. Whether it's a speck or a plank depends on whom you're talking to. Jesus seemed to think the plank was in the eye of the guy who pointed out the other person's flaws.

By the way, this can work both ways. Black people can sometimes be just as quick as white people to point out the plank in their brother's or sister's eye. Our point here is not to try and sort out who has the speck in her eye and who has the plank. Every sin, regardless of size, ultimately works to dehumanize people and marginalize God. White people and black people and every other kind of people are equally in need of God's grace.

What we're saying here is that the speck and plank game does nothing to solve the problem of racism and all its related issues. On the contrary, specks and planks make it worse. It further polarizes people. When black people employ the speck and plank strategy, they are investing energy in accusation rather than reconciliation.[1]

> *Every sin, regardless of size, ultimately works to dehumanize people and marginalize God.*

When white people play at specks and planks, it takes us back to the Jim Crow days, when separation between white and black people was justified in part by a moral critique of the black community.

The shrieking irony in all of this is that a lot of speck-and-plank people, regardless of color, are also Jesus followers. This is ironic because it's Jesus Himself who makes it obvious that focusing on another person's sin does nothing to help us with our own. There is no time to play with specks and planks for the woman or man who is committed to following Jesus. Reconciliation is hard enough as it is without making the gap we are trying to bridge grow even wider. Most of the time, planks are used to build bridges, but not this time.

White people will sometimes push back on all this. When asked to consider the idea that critiquing the black community is merely a way to try and avoid their own culpability, they say, "What do you mean? What plank are you talking about? I don't hate black people. I don't use the *n*-word. I've never knowingly excluded black people from anything because of their race. So what exactly are you talking about? If there's still a racial problem in this country, it's not my fault!"

Well, that's not exactly true.

In chapter 5, we introduced the concept of systemic racism. Our point was that there are certain economic and social systems operating in this country that work against the best interests of the black community. The economic gap between black people and white people and the disproportionate percentage of black people in prison were two examples we cited. Here's the thing about those systems: in a democracy, the people of a country are responsible for the laws and systems that

> *In answer to the protests on the lips of so many white people who say, "This is not my fault!" we must respectfully disagree. In a democracy such as ours, it's on us.*

shape that country's corporate life. That is the genius of our Constitution. It formed a country where the government is of the people, by the people, and for the people.[2] So, if there is an unjust system in our country, it is because "we the people" have allowed it to be here. As a result, in answer to the protests on the lips of so many white people who say, "This is not my fault!" we must respectfully disagree. In a democracy such as ours, it's on us; and the danger is that every time you and I conclude that we have no responsibility for the laws and systems that govern our country, democracy takes a small step backward.

There is some very good news in all this. Because we live in a democracy, we can change things. What's wrong in our country can be set right. The systems that rob people of a fair chance at a good life can be modified or eliminated. There will be naysayers in all this, people who suggest that it is naive to think such deeply entrenched economic and social systems can be changed. They were there 240 years ago when we decided to declare our independence from Britain. They were there when the fight for women's suffrage

> *Because we live in a democracy, we can change things. What's wrong in our country can be set right.*

was enjoined early in the twentieth century. And they are there laughing at us now. But the truth is, this kind of change is not naive. It's just very hard.

That being the case, we cannot allow our energy to be siphoned off by playing the game of specks and planks. While we are busy blaming each other, people are continuing to suffer. While we attempt to comfort ourselves by imagining that our brother's or sister's sin is worse than ours, people are losing ground. You've heard the phrase "Nero fiddled while Rome burned"? At least Nero made music. The noise we make is that of angry people shouting accusations at each other. We can do better. We must do better.

DISCUSSION QUESTIONS

1. This chapter explains the reason why people indulge in the specks-and-planks "game." How would you explain why that behavior occurs?

2. Why do church people attempt to minimize their personal guilt using specks and planks rather than relying upon God's grace?

3. John and Teesha suggest that sometimes white people point to the moral failures of the black community because deep down inside they feel some sense of culpability for the racial injustice in our country. Do you agree? Why or why not?

4. To live in a democracy is to affirm that the people are ultimately responsible for the laws and systems that govern a country. How broadly based should the responsibility be for some of the systemic racism that still exists in our country?

5. There are always naysayers who suggest that change is impossible. These naysayers suggest that specks and planks don't really matter because changing systems that are racially unjust is virtually impossible. Are they right?

Chapter Twelve

THE SUMMER OF '16

"My God, my God, why have you forsaken me?"

—*Jesus (Matthew 27:46)*

I (Teesha) am a native Floridian who later moved to Atlanta, Georgia, and then to Southern California. When I think of summer, I think of warmer temperatures, summer festivals, and time outside with friends. The summer of 2016 had all of those elements but with an unwelcome and in many ways painful addition. That was the summer I watched cell phone video footage of Minnesota police officer Jeronimo Yanez shooting Philando Castile, a black man, during a traffic stop. The video was taken by Philando's girlfriend, Diamond Reynolds, who was also in the car. I can still hear the pop of the officer's gun and see the blood spreading across the front of Philando's bright white T-shirt. I can hear the disbelief and desperation in Diamond's voice as she says, "Oh my God, please don't tell me he's dead." Later in the video, you can hear Diamond wailing as her four-year-old daughter consoles her, saying, "It's okay, Mommy. It's okay, I'm right here with you." An event that is already horrific is made even worse with the realization that a small child saw the entire thing from the backseat. Philando died later that day.

Even after seeing such a graphic video, it can still be easy for us to view these events from a place of separation, to hold Philando and his story at arm's length, and to see this as just another news clip. In other words, it can be easy to forget that Philando was a person. Philando was thirty-two years old when he died. Had he survived the shooting, he would have turned thirty-three just ten days later. A native of St. Louis, he had worked for the St. Paul Public School District for fourteen years as a nutrition services assistant and later as a nutrition services supervisor. His family and friends described him as cheerful and a team player, loved by the students he served.[1] Philando was a person, fearfully and wonderfully made, bearing the image of God.

The horror of seeing Philando shot and killed on July 6, 2016, was intensified by the death of Alton Sterling the day before. On July 5, Alton, also a black man, was shot by police in Baton Rouge, Louisiana. Videos of the shooting were all over the news and social media. Little did I know that the day *after* the image of Philando's blood-soaked shirt was seared into my mind, we would all be faced with yet another atrocity. On July 7, 2016, "during a protest of the killings of Sterling and Castile, Michael Xavier Johnson ambushed and killed five Dallas police officers."[2] The circumstances of these three events were different. Philando and Alton were civilians shot during their interactions with the police. In Dallas, police officers were the victims. Although the specific events surrounding these incidents may have been different, they were still very much connected in my mind and, I think, in the minds of many Americans. All of the events involved tragic loss of life, and race seemed to be a painful common thread. Too many people received the gut-wrenching news that their father, brother, husband, or boyfriend would not be coming home. My soul ached for all of those left behind to mourn and attempt to pick up the pieces.

You do not have to be related to those who have lost their lives in seemingly senseless ways to experience pain. The pain of one should be experienced by all of us. In his letter to the Roman church, Paul writes, "Rejoice with those who rejoice, weep with those who weep" (Romans 12:15). Paul's instruction here is part of an effort to paint a picture of what it means to be a follower of Jesus, not to be "conformed to this world, but be transformed by the renewing of your mind" (Romans 12:2 NASB). According to Paul, one of the marks of being a Christian is a communal experience of pain where the pain of one person is felt by the whole community. Because those who loved Philando, and the many others who died as he did, weep for him, we should also weep.

This communal experience of pain should also flow from our belief in God as creator. As Christians, we believe God is the creator of all things. God's very breath is in our lungs, and God's very image is on each of us (Genesis 1:27). Because Philando (and all who have died tragically as he did) is a human being into whom God breathed the breath of life and who bore the image of God, we should all grieve his death. To grieve Philando's death is an expression of a belief in the sanctity of life.

> *One of the marks of being a Christian is a communal experience of pain where the pain of one person is felt by the whole community.*

In spite of Paul's call to radical empathy and a belief in the sanctity of life as God's good creation, some will respond to the death of black men at the hands of police with skepticism or even contempt. Some will say that Philando, and black men like him, must have done something to deserve their own execution. Some will search these men's pasts, scrutinizing their family life and criminal records, for reasons to justify their deaths. They will dissect each case, looking for fault on the part of the dead or injured person. They will remind their Facebook friends or Twitter followers of the crime rates in the black community.

We must begin to see these responses as contrary to the Christian faith. When our first response to the death or injury of black men and women during interactions with the police is to excuse and explain, we fail to respond scripturally. The scriptural response to the pain of these fellow human beings is to weep and mourn with the families who lost a loved one and with members of the larger black community who go about their everyday lives in fear.

You may recall that lament is the name scripture gives to the communal expression of mourning in response to suffering. We talked about lament in chapter 10 as a necessary part of any effort to "fess up" in the path toward racial reconciliation. Lament is also necessary for our spiritual health and growth as we respond to racist systems and events. There is an insidious tendency in the American church to avoid expressing pain to God, to one another, and even to ourselves. For a person of color, this can mean putting on a mask of strength when, beneath, you are crumbling, angry, afraid, and unsure in the face of rampant racial injustice. For a white person, this can mean going to great lengths to avoid talking about or even seeing the pain of others that results from experiences of racial injustice. Lament gives people of color a means of expressing their deepest fears and even anger to God. In lament, there is freedom to shake your fist at God, to be grieved and broken before God. God invites us to bring our whole selves before God, the wounded and tender parts too. As white people lament and cry out to God on behalf of those experiencing injustice, they place themselves alongside those on the margins and join their appeals to God for peace. Lament connects us to one another. Through lament, we become a people who do not just look at the pain and death brought about by racism, explain it away, and then move on. We become a people who see, and cannot unsee, the ways in which lives have been destroyed by racial injustice. We bring our appeals before God, who is sovereign, and are compelled to engage in the work God is already doing to bring about *shalom*, peace.

When we lament, we are in pretty good company. Jesus lamented. We generally think that if Jesus did it, we should at least give it a try. To be sure, Jesus had good reason to lament. Judas, one of His disciples who had traveled with Him during His public ministry, witnessed Jesus perform miracles, and heard His teaching, betrayed Him for money. Jesus was arrested in front of a large crowd like a common criminal. Then the rest of His trusted disciples abandoned Him. One of the disciples, Peter, denied even knowing Jesus three times, an undoubtedly painful event that Jesus saw coming. It was customary to release a prisoner at the request of the people, but the people chose to release a notorious prisoner, Barabbas, instead. Sealing Jesus's fate, they chanted, "Crucify him! Crucify him!" He was then beaten, taunted, spat on, and made

> *There is an insidious tendency in the American church to avoid expressing pain to God, to one another, and even to ourselves.*

to carry the very wooden beam to which He would be nailed. On the cross, after having endured all of this, Jesus cried out, "My God, my God, why have you forsaken me?" (Matthew 27:46). These are not random words. They are the opening words of Psalm 22, a psalm of lament. When Jesus spoke those words on the cross, He was invoking all of Psalm 22, in all of its rawness and pain, but also in a belief that the one who hears our prayers has the power to answer them. Lament is the scriptural response to pain, our pain and the pain of others. When things are not as they should be, when there is injustice, it is right to tell God in prayer. It is right to cry out to God for peace, equality, and justice.

If lament is not your natural response to pain, the pain of others, or the existence of injustice in the world, how might you start lamenting? The good news is we have a book of prayers of lament that Christians have been using to give voice to injustice for two thousand years. They are not hollow prayers. There are no euphemisms. These prayers flow from places of deep pain and loss. In Psalm 82, the psalmist says, "'How long will you judge unjustly and show partiality to the wicked? Give justice to the weak and the orphan; maintain the right of the lowly and destitute.'" Psalm 82 ends with the powerful plea, "Rise up, O God." Psalm 83 begins, "O God, do not keep silence; do not hold your peace or be still, O God!"

If the psalms do not resonate with you or clearly give voice to your prayers, try writing your own. For a self-professed creative, writing a psalm of lament is a welcome task. For others, it may sound like a bit of a chore. It might just be transformational, so why not give it a try? Spend some time reading psalms of lament. Then spend some time in prayer. Think about a particular person in your community who has shared their experience of racial injustice with you. Think about your own experience of racial injustice. Ask God to help you find the words. Make some space for writing and see what happens. You might surprise yourself. As you build relationships with those who are different from you, listen well to their experiences and lament. Bring injustice before God and ask God to "rise up!"

Lament changes our relationship with one another and with God. Lament, whether it is a response to our pain or to the pain of those with whom we are in relationship, creates a cycle of empathy. As we grow in relationship with those who are different from us, we begin to love them more deeply. As we

> *Lament changes our relationship with one another and with God.*

love more deeply, their pain becomes our pain. When their pain becomes our pain, we must lament. We must cry out to God on their behalf. The cycle of empathy comes full circle because as we lament, our love for our friend grows even deeper. This time it is enriched by divine power. Lament is an expression of pain to be sure, but it is also a request for God to break in and set things right. Friendship drives us toward love. Love compels us to lament. Lament activates a deeper friendship sustained and animated by the power of God. If we leave lament out of our regular rhythms and Christian practice, our capacity for empathy will be stunted and anemic. Lament is the antidote for anemic empathy. It is the vehicle through which the Holy Spirit works to draw us ever closer to one another. Anemic empathy for our neighbor is not the mark of love. We are called to so much more. If Christians are to obey Christ's command to " 'love your neighbor as yourself,' " anemic empathy is woefully insufficient (Matthew 22:39). Empathy cultivated by lament is essential to the sort of friendship that disrupts racism and compels engagement in the work of justice.

DISCUSSION QUESTIONS

1. This chapter starts by recounting the death of Philando Castile, who was shot by a police officer, and, the very next day, the deaths of five Dallas police officers who were shot by a sniper. How did the news of those deaths affect you? Was your response to Mr. Castile's death different than your response to the deaths of the five Dallas police officers? How so?

2. Are you familiar with the practice of lament? How would you explain it to someone who was new to the practice? Teesha and John say lament connects us to one another. How does that work?

3. How do you cultivate a sense of lament for somebody you've never met? How can you make an emotional connection with someone whose path you've never crossed?

4. In the psalms, David expresses lament in a way that sometimes involves critiquing what God has or has not done. Why is it okay to question God in this way?

Chapter Thirteen

THIS IS A FOOTBALL

We have preached a gospel that leaves us believing that we can be reconciled to God but not reconciled to our Christian brothers and sisters who don't look like us.

—*John M. Perkins*

Vince Lombardi is best known for his time as the coach for the Green Bay Packers, though he did have a brief stint as a coach for the Washington Redskins. Lombardi had a remarkable record of six NFL championships and two Super Bowl wins. He was named NFL Coach of the Year twice and was inducted into the Green Bay Packers Hall of Fame. Even the Super Bowl trophy was named after him. Anyone who makes a trip to Lambeau Field, where the Packers play, can't miss the larger-than-life bronze statue of Lombardi that towers over fans.

Even though Lombardi's career was indisputably successful, the

Packers weren't always a winning team. Early in Lombardi's tenure with the Packers, winning an NFL championship remained out of their grasp. Lombardi needed to turn things around. Coming off a tough loss the prior season, Lombardi came to training camp with a new plan. He gave a speech to his players in which he held up a football and said, "Gentlemen, this is a football." He wasn't trying to insult his team or be condescending. He wasn't trying to scold them or imply they were stupid. He was reminding them of what was at the core of their sport, the football. Lombardi needed to set the team on a new course. It turns out that he didn't do it by implementing something new. Instead, he called their attention to something old. He called his team back to the fundamentals.

If we are going to disrupt racism in ways that transform people's realities, then we need to be called back to the fundamentals. As Christians, this means calling our attention back to the gospel and ordering our whole lives around the truth that it communicates. Paul says, "I decided to know nothing among you except Jesus Christ and him crucified" (1 Corinthians 2:2). Paul is holding fast to the fundamentals. Instead of "this is a football," our mantra is "this is the cross."

> *If we are going to disrupt racism in ways that transform people's realities, then we need to be called back to the fundamentals.*

In this chapter, we will explore the biblical rationale for seeking racial reconciliation and disrupting racism in all its forms. What does it mean for antiracism work to be grounded in the cross of Christ?

First, let's address a few fallacies about seeking racial justice. Most of us have probably heard Christians say that seeking racial justice is just a liberal issue or part of the liberal agenda. This is sometimes followed with an argument that disrupting racism is part of the work of "social justice warriors," as they are not so affectionately called. In some Christian circles, just mentioning race will cause you to be labeled as divisive. Some Christians argue that just talking about race is working *against* the kingdom of God because achieving color-blindness is the ultimate virtue. For these Christians, faith in Christ is a spiritual matter where they are predominantly, if not solely, concerned with conversion or "saving souls."

The truth is that pursuing racial justice is—or should be—a nonpartisan project. It is not about whether you support the Democratic or Republican party. It's not about whether you identify as a liberal or a conservative. We must choose this day whom we will serve. Will we serve power, wealth, and comfort, or will we serve Christ (see Matthew 6:24)? You cannot do both. When we raise these straw-man arguments that place racial justice work outside the reach of the gospel, we reject Christ.

Dietrich Bonhoeffer was a German theologian and pastor who was imprisoned and executed for participating in a movement to overthrow Adolf Hitler. In a sermon he gave in Barcelona for Advent, Bonhoeffer said, "Christ walks on earth as your neighbor as long as there are people." We encounter Jesus in "complete reality" as the "ruined human being in torn clothing" seeking help. Christ comes to us as those who are different, as those who exist at the margins. Bonhoeffer challenged his listeners, "Will you keep the door locked or open it to him?"[1] Racial justice is not a distraction from the gospel or the work of the church. It is the gospel. The gospel has both spiritual and concrete manifestations. When the people of God work to bring about racial justice, it's one way we know that Christ is risen and the

Holy Spirit has been poured out, ushering in a new way of being and relating to one another in the world.

We have already looked at how failing to engage in issues of racial justice will adversely impact the credibility of the church and our ability to provide moral leadership on issues of race. But even if there was no pragmatic reason for the church to address racism, Christians would still be called to do it because God is in the business of reconciling people to God's self and to one another.

> *Racial justice is not a distraction from the gospel or the work of the church. It is the gospel.*

Christians believe that, through Jesus, God came to be with us as a human being. Theologians call this the *incarnation*. It is a glorious yet surprising part of our faith. Christ entered a world that did not reflect God's intention, a world full of sinful people who created sinful systems where power, wealth, lust, and violence reigned supreme. But Jesus's coming ushered in a radically new way of ordering all aspects of society. This is what Jesus meant when He proclaimed that the "kingdom of God has come near" (Mark 1:15 NIV). Jesus called people to turn away from their old ways of living and ordering society and to choose instead to believe this good news. In this new world order that Jesus preached, in the kingdom of God, the last would be first, the meek would inherit the earth, weakness was strength, and wealth afforded no privilege. Jesus preached sermons and told parables about this new kingdom that belonged to God, not Caesar.

Even Jesus's miracles pointed to the coming of the kingdom of God. He performed miracles that restored into community those whom society had cast out. The Gospel of John uses a Greek word that means "sign" to refer to Jesus's miracles. Like a sign, Jesus's miracles point us to Jesus's divine power and His intention to bring those on the outside, in. The kingdom of God has come near. Of course, Jesus's message and intention were not welcomed by everyone. Those with political and religious power and wealth deemed Jesus's message heretical and seditious. The state tortured and murdered Jesus by nailing Him to a cross. There can be no doubt that, through Jesus, God was doing a new thing, because Jesus took upon Himself the sin of the world and laid down His life. Jesus suffered and died on a Roman cross like a common criminal. All that Jesus had been preaching is imaged in this event. In this suffering God nailed to a cross, we are saved. When Jesus took His last breath, the curtain in the temple that separated us from the Holy of Holies, where God dwelled, was torn in two (Mark 15:38). There was no longer any separation between the people and God. We know that the story of Jesus does not end there. After being dead for three days, Jesus was resurrected, proving once and for all that Jesus is Lord. Jesus's life, death, and resurrection have implications for our relationship with God and with one another. Through Christ, "the veil was torn" so that there was no barrier to the Holy of Holies, the place of God's presence. In Christ, we can be reconciled to God, but that is only part of the good news. Jesus's coming means the kingdom of God has come near, and through this kingdom, God calls us to a radical reordering of society and relationships. In Christ, we can be reconciled to one another.

Look at how God's purpose to reconcile people to God's self and to one another played out in the church in Ephesus, where ethnic and religious differences caused division in the church. Race did not function in precisely the same way in the ancient Greco-Roman world as it does in the United States. In the ancient Near Eastern/

Mediterranean world, people did not create hierarchies based solely on the color of one's skin. For the ancient Jewish people, group identity was grounded primarily in religion.[2] Those who did not share in the Jewish faith by worshiping the God of Abraham, Isaac, and Jacob were outsiders.[3] Thus, the Jew/Gentile divide concerned characteristics that raised real questions about who was in and who was out, who would be counted among the people of God and who would not. The divide addressed in Ephesians 2:11-22 provides a good analogy for today's racial divisions and gives us some clues about God's intention when such divisions arise.

Paul begins by pointing out that those who were Gentiles from birth were outside of God's covenantal promise to Abraham. However, God did not leave the Gentiles this way. Verse 13 says, "But now in Christ Jesus you who once were far off have been brought near by the blood of Christ" (NRSV). The words "but now" are beautiful. They signal a shift, a hard right turn, a plot twist. The Gentiles were once far from God, but now (plot twist), through Christ, they have been brought near. In Christ's saving act on the cross, Jews and Gentiles alike were reconciled, brought near, to God. But Christ's death and resurrection did not only impact their relationship with God. Verse 14 says, "in [Jesus's] flesh he has made both groups into one and has broken down the dividing wall, that is, the hostility between us"

> *Working against racism is part of what it means to call Jesus Lord and Savior. Racism is opposed to God's desire for all people to be reconciled to one another in one body that is reconciled to God.*

(NRSV). Through the cross, God created "one new humanity," reconciling these two groups of different ethnic and religious origins to one another.

So, here's where we land. We have to return to the fundamentals and let our mantra be "this is the cross." God invites us to live into the story of divine and interpersonal reconciliation through the cross of Christ. With Christ's death, the veil that separated us from God's dwelling place, the Holy of Holies, was torn. But so were the walls and hostility that separate us because of our racial and ethnic differences. We exist as a beautiful array of races, cultures, and ethnicities. In our difference, we can be united as one body because of Christ's work on the cross. Absent these walls, we are free for one another. We are free to love one another in tangible expressions of Christ's love. What does that look like? It looks like the kingdom of God has come near. It looks like Christians working to bring about the new world order that Jesus preached—in our personal lives and in the systems under which we live. Working against racism is part of what it means to call Jesus Lord and Savior. Racism is opposed to God's desire for all people to be reconciled to one another in one body that is reconciled to God. The kingdom of God has come near, and that is really good news.

DISCUSSION QUESTIONS

1. In this chapter Teesha and John suggest that the work of disrupting racism is not a departure from the foundations of our faith but is actually based on those foundations. How do you feel about that?

2. Jesus spent a lot of time with people who were marginalized by the religious authorities found in first-century Israel. He was critiqued for doing so. Today, marginalization is a common tactic when racism is at work. Do you think people who spend time with those who have been racially marginalized are likely to face the same kind of pushback Jesus did?

3. What can we learn about disrupting racism from the way Paul handled the divide between Jews and Gentiles in the first century?

4. If you're working through the discussion questions in chapter 13, then congratulations! You've put in a lot of time reading this book so far. As you digest its contents, has your thinking about racial issues changed? How so?

Chapter Fourteen

LAND OF OPPORTUNITY

*We have also come to this hallowed spot to remind America of the
fierce urgency of now. . . . Now is the time to make real the promises
of democracy.*

—*Martin Luther King Jr.*

Afriend recently went to an event where the community filled
an arena to watch various equestrian events. There were cute
miniature horses, and a few Clydesdales made an appearance. At one
point during the event, the American flag was brought out and the
national anthem and other patriotic songs were played. A single horse
without a rider entered the arena in honor of first responders who had
died in service to the community. As my friend recalled this moment
of shared national pride and perhaps mourning, you could see the
emotion well up inside him. For him, to be American is a source of
pride. The American flag and the national anthem are symbols of

freedom and greatness. They represent what is true, beautiful, and good. He isn't wrong. It just doesn't represent the whole picture of America for all Americans.

Some people have an ambivalent relationship with the United States. To be American is not a reason for pride. For some, particularly people of color, their perception of America is rife with complexities. It can cause a feeling of ambivalence. The national anthem, the American flag, and the bald eagle are not necessarily symbols that conjure up feelings of patriotism or joy. For others, people like my friend, these symbols carry great importance and are deserving of high esteem. For them, America may be the greatest country on the earth and being American is an identity that ought to be claimed as a badge of honor.

How do we manage the apparent conflicts between these two perceptions of America? Faithfulness requires that we live in the tension between irreparable shame and unquestioning pride. If we attempt to resolve this tension by wholeheartedly choosing one side over another, we risk affirming a belief in an ineffectual Christ who cannot redeem on the one hand and a Christ who is willing to share our praise with mere idols on the other.

The United States has a shameful history of oppressing, stealing from, and generally committing violence toward nonwhite people. Black Africans were kidnapped from their homes and

> *How do we manage the apparent conflicts between these two perceptions of America? Faithfulness requires that we live in the tension between irreparable shame and unquestioning pride.*

sold like livestock to perform grueling work on plantations through-out the South. Slaves were beaten and raped, and families were sepa-rated from one another. All of this was entirely legal and was done in the name of economic prosperity and white racial superiority.

Racism was written into America's founding. The Declaration of Independence boldly and righteously declares that, "We hold these truths to be self-evident, that all men are created equal, that they are endowed by their Creator with certain unalienable Rights, that among these are Life, Liberty, and the pursuit of Happiness." These words express an unequivocal belief in the inherent value of all humans. By virtue of this inherent value that is given by God, all humans have certain rights that are "unalienable," which means they cannot be taken away by a person or government. Yet while the words of the Declaration of Independence may be clear, compelling, and powerful, they are not consistent with the conduct of many of its signatories and America's other founders. Thomas Jefferson, the principal author of the Declaration of Independence and the third president of the United States, was a slaveholder. Even the first president of the United States, George Washington, was a slaveholder.

The political prerogatives of the slave owners among Founding Fathers shaped the Constitution of the United States. According to Article I, Section 2 of the Constitution, only a free person could be counted as a whole person for the purpose of determining representation in the House of Representatives; slaves were counted as only three-fifths of a person. It took a constitutional amendment (the thirteenth, ratified in 1865) to render black Americans as whole persons. Though this book is primarily focused on friendship and power between black Americans and white Americans, we would be remiss if we did not note that people of African descent were not the only people treated shamefully by the white founders of the

United States. The case of indigenous peoples, who have inhabited the country we now call home far longer than any person of European descent, were subject to a genocide when European colonists first took the land now known as the United States. Those indigenous people who survived were forcibly removed from their homes and compelled to undertake arduous and lengthy journeys to relocate to designated areas. Such relocation, war, and enslavement led to the decimation of the indigenous populations.[1]

We could go on. But suffice it to say that for many, America's past makes love of country difficult. Many nonwhite people hear the national anthem at a baseball game and think, *America has never loved me, so how can I love America?*

And it is not only America's past that is an obstacle to some people's ability to fully embrace the label "patriot." People of color must also contend with how patriotism is used against them today. Love of country is often employed as a cudgel, a tool to silence criticisms of the United States by people of color, particularly when those criticisms center on race relations. Consider the controversy surrounding the NFL players who kneel during the national anthem to protest police brutality and racism. Both the media and political pundits portray their actions as anti-American. Those who oppose kneeling during the national anthem believe, among other things, that it is a show of disrespect to the United States and those who serve in the military. In contrast, those who kneel would say that they are not protesting the national anthem, the United States as a whole, or our military. Rather, they kneel to bring attention to the issue of police brutality against black men and women.

> *For many, America's past makes love of country difficult.*

Whatever your opinion on NFL players' choice to kneel during the national anthem, this symbol of America and the feeling of patriotism it is supposed to induce are used to silence the voices of those who wish to expose racism. For people who disapprove of kneeling, there is no satisfactory reason to kneel during the national anthem. Respect for the symbols of America is of paramount importance. Such respect, for them, takes precedence over highlighting the loss of life or liberty experienced by black people.

In this way, patriotism is a silencer. It is a way for some people to say to the NFL players, "Shut up and play." When patriotism is used to squelch efforts to highlight racial injustice, many black Americans begin to wonder about the genuineness of this patriotism. It can be difficult to align with people who seem chiefly interested in your silence.

Yet even as the history of the United States is abhorrent in many ways, the Declaration of Independence and Constitution do express ideals toward which the country can still strive. The preamble to the Constitution says that the document is promulgated by "We the People of the United States." That's us. We are the ones being called to live into the values that follow. Among the stated reasons the Constitution was written and ratified was to "establish Jus-

> *When patriotism is used to squelch efforts to highlight racial injustice, many black Americans begin to wonder about the genuineness of this patriotism.*

tice," "promote the general Welfare," and "secure the Blessings of Liberty to ourselves and our Posterity." Similarly, the Declaration of Independence assumes a Divine creator who gives all people the right to

"Life, Liberty and the pursuit of Happiness," a right which the government cannot take away. There can be no doubt that the United States has fallen and continues to fall short of these expressed ideals. However, the fact that we as a nation have thus far failed to fully embody our stated values is no reason not to continue the fight to "establish Justice." These words of the founding documents are unambiguous and should propel us forward. They create space in the political sphere to pursue racial justice in an effort to call the United States up to the standards upon which it was founded.

In his famous "I Have a Dream" speech delivered at the March on Washington for Jobs and Freedom in 1963, Martin Luther King Jr. used a vivid metaphor to call the United States to account in the area of race relations. He did not seek to discard America's founding documents. He asked America to finally embody the ideals the Founders expressed. King argued that they had come to Washington, DC, to "cash a check." He was not referring to a physical check for a particular dollar amount. He argued that in writing "the Constitution and the Declaration of Independence, the Founders were writing a promissory note to every American" of all races. By this promissory note, all Americans are guaranteed an inalienable right to life, liberty, and the pursuit of happiness. But America was in default on this promissory note with respect to its citizens of color. So, King said, "We've come to cash this check." He refused to believe that the "bank of justice [was] bankrupt." In other

> *In writing "the Constitution and the Declaration of Independence, the Founders were writing a promissory note to every American" of all races.*

words, there was still time for America to live up to the standard it had set for itself because "now is the time to make real the promises of democracy."[2] King's words ring true even today.

Americans ought not take naive comfort in the noble ideals expressed in our founding documents. Yet, if we choose to dwell exclusively on the violent and racist past of the United States, we may descend into an incurable bitterness. What's worse, we may lose sight of God's power to redeem our history and transform our country in ways that we can hardly imagine.

We should become deeply aware of the history of this country so that we might, as a nation, turn from white supremacy and its hold on our systems. However, the past cannot be all we see. We must also turn our gaze toward God, who is at work redeeming all things. Focused on God, we can allow ourselves to criticize America, not because we hate it but precisely because we love it, see it for what it is, and see it for what it could be.

DISCUSSION QUESTIONS

1. What is your view of Thomas Jefferson and George Washington? How do you hold together the noble and self-sacrificial things they did with their slave-owning?

2. John and Teesha make the point that real patriotism makes room for critiquing the country we love, hoping that such criticism will make it the best it can be. How can you tell the difference between a critique that helps our country and a critique that harms our country?

3. How can we engage in a conversation about racism in the United States with those who disagree with us without becoming bitter enemies?

Chapter Fifteen

IT'S TRICKY

What is it about the institution of a denomination or church that seems to repel people who are different?

—Christena Cleveland

We encounter race, racism, and the unfinished quest for racial justice in all corners of our lives—at our workplaces, at the grocery store, at birthday parties, at the bank. We also encounter them at church—and that's what this chapter is about. How does racial reconciliation play out in our churches?

As we thought about this, we realized we could write a whole book about it. We could write about the regrettable history of racism in the church. We could, conversely, write about how the church sometimes stood against racism. We could write about the relationship between the church and the world of politics. We could write about the relationship between working for racial justice and evangelism. But we decided to write about just one aspect of this issue. We decided to write about racially integrating the local church. In some ways, this seems like ground zero. If our congregations aren't integrated, how can Christians speak with any integrity in the ongoing public discourse about race and racism? On the surface, integrating congregations seems like the obvious thing to do, but we discovered this is a tricky thing to try.

To begin, we need to ask a foundational question: Should Christians always seek to integrate their churches? And we need to ask a second, similar question: Should Christians always seek to worship in churches that are racially integrated or actively working on becoming racially integrated? These are complicated questions because a church's racial composition should reflect the racial composition of the community in which it exists. In other words, the optimal racial configuration of a congregation is contextual. It's going to look different in different situations. As a result, sometimes an all-black church makes sense. But we can seldom say the same thing about an all-white church.

We realize this is precisely the sort of claim that makes some white Christians feel defensive or annoyed. How can we suggest that all-black churches are sometimes appropriate, but all-white churches almost never are? Our argument is this: certain historical and socio-

> **Should Christians always seek to integrate their churches?**

logical circumstances called all-black churches into being, and similar circumstances warrant their continued flourishing today. The black church was created out of necessity. White people wouldn't allow black people to worship alongside them, wouldn't allow black people to be ordained or to hold any sort of leadership role. No such restrictions were ever placed on white people by their black brothers and sisters.

As a result, black people felt like they had to start their own churches and denominations. It was a matter of being faithful to what God called them to do. These communities became places for black people to exercise their spiritual gifts and vocations in a way that was denied them in the white church. But there were other reasons that made all-black churches essential for the black community.

Black churches provided a space where black Americans were able to politically organize. Many of the meetings where the civil rights activists of the 1950s and 1960s made their plans were held in black church social halls. White Christians had plenty of other places to politically organize. There was no other such place for black Americans.

All-black churches provided a place for black people to "let their hair down." They were safe places where the beleaguered black community could experience healing, where their community could be nurtured, and where black people could reacquire the joy of being who God had made them to be. They could socialize without having to endure a polite conversation with a well-meaning white person who was going to inadvertently insult them.

> *Because racism is still active in our country, the black church is still active. The first all-black churches provided shelter from the storm. That shelter is still needed.*

White Christians never needed and still don't need an all-white church to provide these benefits. But black churches were needful, and sadly the need for all-black churches is still with us today. Because racism is still active in our country, the black church is still active. The first all-black churches provided shelter from the storm. That shelter is still needed.

This reality makes the idea of an integrated church tricky. On the surface, it would seem that an integrated church is always the best option. But the presence of ongoing racism means that sometimes this is not the case. That said, we are both involved in racially integrated congregations: one in Atlanta, Georgia, and one in Pasadena, California.

Our experience has shown us that life inside an integrated church is complicated—wonderfully, maddeningly, blessedly complicated. Things sometimes feel fragile. Platitudes and simplistic answers don't help. Trying to knit together a white community and a black community after all that's happened between the two over the past four hundred years is no walk in the park. Here are a couple of case studies, beyond our own circumstances, that illustrate what we mean.

St. John's is a church in a medium-sized metropolitan area in the Midwest; it has seen a growing number of black people in attendance over the last eight years.[1] This church began in 1848 and was virtually all white for most of its existence. But in 2012, a predominantly black church in the area suffered the loss of its pastor due to a moral crisis. A sizable number of people left that church. As it turned out, a lot of those people started coming to this predominantly white church. They had a positive experience there. This drew in other black people who also had a positive experience. By 2016, people of color represented 15 to 20 percent of the congregation.

The director of music at this church (who was white) was 100 percent behind this trend. She realized, however, that the church choir tended to sing hymns that reflected a very white cultural heritage. To make the church's musical offerings more accessible to an increasingly diverse congregation, she started to add some more gospel-oriented music to what was sung. The quality of the music was good. The reaction from the congregation, however, was mixed.

Perhaps it comes as no surprise that most of the black people in the congregation were excited about singing hymns that reflected their cultural background. They connected with these songs. Singing "Precious Lord" and "He's Able" enhanced their worship experience. That said, some of the black people were almost insulted. They felt that the choir director had made assumptions based on stereotypes. Did she think they liked gospel music just because they were black? The choir director had to scramble to assure these people that no insult was intended. But she kept those songs in the hymn rotation.

Then there was the response from some of the white people.

Most of the white people in the congregation adapted to gospel songs like "He's Able." If pressed, they might have admitted the new (to them) songs weren't their first love, but they realized the value of diversity and didn't make a big deal about it. Some enjoyed the musical change in style as it allowed them to worship God in fresh ways. Other white people, however, grew increasingly uncomfortable not only with the new musical selections but perhaps with the sense that they were losing control over their Sunday service. Their connection with the church began to loosen. They stopped coming regularly. Some left. The director of music was able to sit down with one of the white people who'd cut ties with the church. When she inquired about why he left he said, "It just doesn't feel like my church anymore." It turns out that he had begun to attend a predominantly white church where the music was more to his liking.

We heard another story about a majority-black denominational church in the downtown area of a midsized city in the Northeast. In the early 2000s, this church was asked by its denominational headquarters to assume the leadership of a suburban congregation also in that denomination. So, some of the downtown pastors, who were black, were reassigned to this suburban congregation. This suburban church, by the way, was a majority-white congregation, even though the suburb contained a sizable number of black people. The church wasn't growing, but the cultural distance between it and the surrounding community was.

Upon assuming leadership of this suburban church, the newly appointed pastors from the downtown church decided to begin offering a blended style of worship. They wove traditional "white" hymns together with contemporary Christian music and gospel music. There was no gradual shift; the new pastors introduced this blended music on their first Sunday. They asked the white people in the congregation to stay and engage with this new model of worship in the hopes that the blended worship style would do a better job of connecting with the racially blended suburb in which the church was located.

Fast-forward ten years. The church experienced moderate growth. But the racial mix changed from 100 percent white to 30 percent white and 70 percent black. It is important to note that while the church did grow under the new leadership, the fact that it became integrated was fueled as much by white people leaving as it was by new black people coming.

As we think about these two case studies, some important questions arise. To what degree was racism involved in the departure of the white people from these increasingly diverse congregations? Is there a difference between cultural preference and racist bigotry? How would an outside observer know exactly which motive sent those white people on their way? Indeed, how would the congregants themselves fully know? The inner world of a human being where multiple motives swirl around each other is never easy to untangle. We seldom do anything for one simple and clear reason, and it's gut-wrenchingly difficult for us to be honest with ourselves, let alone with others. "The heart is deceitful above all things and beyond cure," says the prophet Jeremiah. "Who can understand it?" (Jeremiah 17:9 NIV).

Divided by Faith, a book by sociologists Michael O. Emerson and Christian Smith, helped us make some sense out of all this. Emerson and Smith pointed out that in the United States, we have the opportunity to choose exactly what we want from a thousand different options, whether we're looking for a new kind of ice cream, a new automobile, or a new church. In other words, Christians in America have become religious consumers.[2]

And what motivates Christians to look for a new church? Any pastor who has been around the block once or twice will tell you that by far and away the most common answer is "I wasn't being fed at my old church." In other words, people want something they aren't getting, and, just like looking for a new pair of shoes or a new car, they go "church shopping." They know there are a plethora of religious choices in their town or city—and their task is simply to shop for a church that's "a better fit" for them.

The research Emerson and Smith did for their book provides some concrete data that illuminates exactly what these "church shoppers" are searching for. It turns out that "not being fed" isn't always a critique of the sermons they hear. "Not being fed" is a catchphrase for a much more nuanced set of preferences. As sociologists, Emerson and Smith understood that religious groups exist to supply members with meaning, belonging, and

> *A satisfying church experience includes feeling like you fit in.*

security.[3] Of particular relevance to our discussion here is the idea of belonging. A satisfying church experience includes feeling like you fit in. And when religious consumers feel like they no longer fit in, they begin to look for a place where they can reacquire that sense of belonging.

Emerson and Smith were curious about what creates a sense of belonging. They noted that, generally speaking, people like to be with people who are like themselves.[4] In other words, Georgia football fans like to be with other Georgia football fans. Musicians like to hang out with other musicians. Moms like to spend time with moms. And, generally speaking, when they want to find a place where they fit in, black people gravitate toward other black people and white people look for other white people. The authors take care to distinguish this from racism. As a result, they arrive at this daunting conclusion: "Merely eliminating racial prejudice would not end racially divided churches."[5]

In light of this, can we avoid the conclusion that attempting to get blacks and whites to sit together in church is a fool's errand? Does it run afoul of basic human nature? Should black Christians point to the white church across town and say, "The Body of Christ is very diverse. Just look at those people over there. They're very different from us. But they are our brothers and sisters in Christ." Should white churches point to the black churches and say, "There is the proof that Jesus Christ is for everybody. Those churches are filled with people who aren't like us at all. But the fact that they are different and yet Christian makes the diversity of the Body of Christ unmissable." So far, that's pretty much what we've got in the American church.

As we noted at the beginning of the chapter, an integrated congregation isn't always going to be the goal. Nonetheless, a growing number of American Christians, including us, want to worship in integrated spaces. Given Smith and Emerson's research, how is our hope not just one colossal unrealistic expectation?

Actually, that's exactly what it is. Unrealistic. If sociology is the only perspective from which we assess this idea of an integrated church, then we are wasting our time. But there is something more than sociology at work here. God is in the business of doing what, by human standards, is unrealistic. It has always been that way.

It was unrealistic for a first-century itinerant Jewish carpenter to predict His own death and resurrection. It was unrealistic for that same carpenter to talk about building a community that could withstand the ravages of time and opposition (Matthew 16:18). And yet here we are, two thousand years later and three billion strong. Were these things unrealistic? Yes. Did they happen? Yes, they did.

As it turns out, when something is unrealistic, when something is tricky, that's when God's transcendent power shines. God specializes in pulling off the unrealistic. So, when we're staring at the unrealistic prospect of seeing the church begin to integrate itself in the United States, we're facing yet another opportunity to see God's transcendent power shine. You might say, "But segregation in the church has been a problem for four hundred years in this country!" You are correct. But God often waits a vexing amount of time

> *When something is unrealistic, when something is tricky, that's when God's transcendent power shines. God specializes in pulling off the unrealistic.*

to do something unrealistic. That, too, seems to be part of the way God works.

What do we do? What follows are three practical suggestions for anyone who wants to see God do, once again, what is unrealistic.

The first thing to do is pray. You've heard this a thousand times. Yet in a culture that demands a quick answer and an instant solution, this is a tough discipline for us to embrace. However, nothing wonderful will happen at your church regarding racial reconciliation apart from prayer. This is the message we hear from Martin Luther King Jr., from William Wilberforce, from Desmond Tutu, from Rosa Parks. Yet we fear that praying might dissuade us from action. On the contrary, prayer is not a substitute for action. It is the foundation upon which action rests. So never pray without acting (James 2:20). And never act without praying (Ephesians 6:18, 1 Thessalonians 5:15).

Second, the place where real integration takes place is not in the pews on Sunday morning. Integration in the pews is essential, but it is not sufficient. The place where integration really takes place is at the table where your church makes decisions. This place will vary from church to church and from denomination to denomination. But if the decisions that govern the life of the congregation are being made in ethnic isolation, then the racial mix in the congregation on Sunday morning is only window dressing that won't last long.

There are numerous reasons for this. At the top of the list is the fact that racial integration is going to look different in different churches. It is not formulaic. It must be organic and authentic. It must be sustainable. This is not possible if the decision-makers are all of a single race. You will need the perspectives of diverse decision-makers to meet the needs of a diverse congregation. This is not a problem for white people to solve by themselves. This is not a problem for black people to solve by themselves. An authentic, organic, and sustainable expression of racial integration cannot be achieved unless both black and white people are participating in the decision-making process. You want to see your church become integrated? Start with the leadership.

Finally, we have to adjust our thinking about how long this will take. Too often, we want integration to be a sprint. We want to work hard for a little while and get it done. But integrating churches is not a sprint. It's a marathon. And even non-runners know that attempting to sprint through a marathon guarantees that you will not finish the race.

Think about it. It takes six months for a church to decide about the color of the new carpet in the sanctuary. Deciding about the color of your congregation is going to take a little longer, and understandably so. We are hopeful, but we are afraid. We want to establish authentic friendships in our church with people who don't look like us, but we don't want to lose who we are in the process. We want the doors of the church to be open to everyone, but when everyone shows up, we realize some things must change. As Harvard professor Ronald Heifetz says, "People don't fear change. They fear loss."[6] We want our church to be diverse, but we don't want to lose our church's familiar, comfortable feeling.

Combine that fear of loss with a little bigotry here, a little anger there, and the way forward starts to feel like a minefield. One wrong step and *Kapow!* No wonder the sociologists say that the prospect of an integrated church is unrealistic.

Well, here's the thing. Our church is not really ours. It's God's. And God intends to shape it to reflect God's amazing love for all people. As the children's song goes, "Red and yellow, black and white, they are precious in His sight." Can we resist God's agenda? Yes. That church building downtown that was converted into a nightclub? The congregation that used to worship there somehow resisted God's agenda. That other church, the one four blocks over from you that was sold and razed so a developer could build some condos? Chances are that church dug in its heels and resisted what God wanted to do in and through them.

When it comes to any issue, resisting the Source of a congregation's life is never a good idea. It's like sawing off the limb upon which you're standing. We might think we're standing on the preaching of an excellent pastor, or on a great youth ministry, or on an attractive facility, but we're not. The only thing that keeps a church vital and alive is the Author of the church. And that ain't us.

> *Our church is not really ours. It's God's. And God intends to shape it to reflect God's amazing love for all people.*

The good news here is that the kingdom of God is not in trouble. It never is. Its power and life flow into communities surrendered to its agenda. If that's not your church's reality right now, don't panic. God is patient. God's mercies are new every morning. But the world is waiting. The clock is ticking. The time to align ourselves with God's vision for a diverse, beloved community is now. As we'll see in the next chapter, that has everything to do with regaining the credibility the church loses when it holds itself apart from the agenda of its Author.

DISCUSSION QUESTIONS

1. How would you describe the demographic makeup of the church you currently attend? Is it predominantly black or white, Asian or Hispanic or Indian? Or is it a mixture of the above? What percentage of the congregation does each of the racial categories above represent?

2. Do you feel like your church accurately reflects the level of diversity that exists in the surrounding community? If so, how did that happen? If not, why didn't that happen? Would you like to see that change?

3. John and Teesha mention a book called *Divided by Faith*. That book points out that cultural preferences and racism are not necessarily the same thing. For example, a preference for black gospel music doesn't necessarily mean you have a racial bias against white people. That said, how do you tell the difference between cultural preferences and racial biases?

4. Do you think every congregation should be diverse? Why?

5. This chapter ends by implying that the larger culture is watching the church to see what it does regarding racial diversity. Do you think that's still true? Or do you think an increasingly secular culture no longer cares what the church does?

Chapter Sixteen

REGAINING CREDIBILITY

I love the pure, peaceable, and impartial Christianity of Christ; I therefore hate the corrupt, slave-holding, women-whipping, cradle-plundering, partial and hypocritical Christianity of this land.

—*Frederick Douglass*

In 2018, Anthony Bourdain, award-winning chef and host of the food travel show *Parts Unknown*, died by suicide. In the days after his death, some Christians took to social media to declare that this celebrity was in hell because he had killed himself. Many outside the church read those posts and tweets in horror, concluding that only heartless people would say such things about a person at all, let alone so soon after his death. So, Christians must be a heartless group of people. Christians must be a people who care more about issuing moral judgments than about addressing people's real pain. They will reason that if Christians are heartless, then their God must also be heartless, uncaring, and primarily concerned with meting out judgment. While this may very well describe some professed Christians, it is a poor description of the God who made us, loves us, and gave God's only Son for us. Yet, it is not hard to see how people can draw these conclusions about God based on the actions of God's followers.

When Christians don't love people well, others assume that God is not loving and that the church is a place where the unloving gather to worship their unloving God. This is the crisis facing the church today when it comes to issues of race. Much of the church has failed to clearly and compassionately address racism in America, and as a result, our credibility is on the line.

Historically, the church has a mixed record when it comes to race and racism. It has both fought against and promulgated racist practices and systems. From the era of slavery to the era of the civil rights movement and beyond, many Christians have opposed the oppression of black people. Yet, on the other hand, Christians have also used Scripture to support the institution of slavery. For example, many Southern slaveholders loved the letter of Philemon—they viewed Paul's returning Onesimus, likely a runaway slave, to his master as a model for contemporary slave owners and a justification for the maintenance of slavery throughout the Southern states. Institutionally, slavery divided churches. The Baptists split over the question of whether slaveowners could serve as denominational missionaries. The Methodists split over the question of whether a bishop could own slaves. In the twentieth century, many northern and southern Christians were apathetic about or actively opposed to efforts of the civil rights movement to bring about racial equality in America. Because the American church has a record that is at best mixed, this chapter may be more appropriately titled "Gaining Credibility."

Whether the church needs to gain credibility for the first time or regain credibility that has been lost, the bottom line is that when it comes to issues of racial justice, much of the church lacks the integrity necessary to lead our country toward racial equality and reconciliation. We know almost instinctively that when Christians behave in a Christlike manner, people are attracted to Christ and to the church. The inverse is also true. How the church responds to the pain of others impacts its credibility as the professed body of Christ. It turns out that apathy in the fight against racism makes the church repellant. When we use the word *church* here, we mean the people of God. We are talking about the everyday actions of Christians, not statements or resolutions drafted by denominational bodies, though these are important. What are the church people in your community actually doing to combat racism?

It's important that Christians work against racism because Jesus is interested in breaking down barriers between people and in combating injustice; but it's also important because Christians who ignore racism are ineffective witnesses for the faith. And it's sad to say that today the broader society cannot necessarily look to the church for practical guidance on how to have cross-racial conversations, bridge divides among the races, or even love those who are different. Not much has changed since Martin Luther King Jr. said that Sunday morning at 11:00 was the most segregated hour in Christian America.[1] The church is a largely segregated institution that is not leading in having difficult conversations about race or combating systemic racism. Christians talk about the love of Christ, the Prince of Peace, but you would never know it based on the church's apathy when it comes to the decidedly unpeaceful racial strife that plagues our country. Many Christians pride themselves on being pro-life. Yet, sometimes we seem to care more about the life of an unborn child than the life of a black person born twenty years ago. We tweet #AllLivesMatter on social media, but we seem to have little care for eighteen-year-old Michael Brown, whose body lay in the middle of the street uncovered and exposed to the elements for hours. Non-Christians are left to wonder which lives Christians are interested in protecting. When our professed faith is inconsistent with our collective actions, the church lacks the credibility to meaningfully impact issues of racial injustice and call others to engage in this work. Our brothers and sisters of color are dying, living in fear, enduring humiliation, and navigating a system that does not contemplate their success. They are crying out, and much of the church is silent.

The church in America should be the first place in the world where God's love and justice are brought to bear on this great evil. As we wait for Christ's return, the vocation of the church is to be the body of Christ. We are Christ made physically visible to the world, except when we are not. When the church fails to engage its vocation as the body of Christ, many Americans will unceremoniously write the church off as irrelevant. It's not uncommon to hear the sentiment "If your church is not interested in fighting racism, then I'm not interested in your church." Even worse is the sentiment "If your God is not interested in fighting racism, then I am not interested in your God." The church's failure to speak out against racism is a clear and direct hindrance to our ability to share the gospel. But when the church is faithful to God by accurately showing what type of person Jesus is, then others just might become curious about God through God's people.

While the church may be losing credibility here in the United States, the church in the global south (Africa, Latin America, and parts of Asia) is flourishing. The kingdom of God is not in danger. God is not pacing back and forth worrying about how to eradicate racism in America because, as the Gospel of John says, "The light shines in the darkness, and the darkness has not overcome it" (1:5). God's kingdom and God's justice will have the last say. We can be assured of that.

> *The church in America should be the first place in the world where God's love and justice are brought to bear on this great evil.*

What we must decide is how brightly we want that light to shine here in the United States. God is ushering in a new heaven and a new earth where people "from every nation, from all tribes and peoples and languages" will be together in worshiping God (Revelation 7:9, 21:1 NRSV). This is the endgame, and God is already at work bringing it about. We can choose to partner with God, or we can sit on the sidelines. The light of racial justice is pretty dim in the United States at present, but it can shine a whole lot brighter. God often works through people, so it's up to us to allow that to happen. We just might be the answer to our own prayers for racial justice.

What is the future of the church in America? If we decide not to be a part of what God is doing to bring about racial justice and reconciliation, it might not be so bright. If the church wants to take a pass on the fight against racism, eventually God will give us what we want. We'll sit on the sidelines wondering why people think our faith is irrelevant. We'll wonder why our church is losing influence. We'll wonder why our communities no longer take us seriously . . . why they really don't think much about us at all. Our church will be on the margins because that's what we asked for—to be allowed to do nothing while one of the most important spiritual battles of the twenty-first century rages all around us. We will see life in our corner of the earth look less and less like heaven. God's kingdom will surge ahead all over the world, but we will not see the same surge here.

But it does not have to happen that way. When we, the church, weigh in on racism in a redemptive and compassionate manner, it can go a long way toward regaining the credibility we've lost.

DISCUSSION QUESTIONS

1. In the eighteenth and first half of the nineteenth centuries, many churches in the United States supported the institution of slavery. Today the church is often apathetic toward racism. How are supporting slavery and being apathetic toward racism similar? How are they different?

2. Why do some Christians find it easier to engage in activism on behalf of an unborn child than on behalf of a black twenty-year-old?

3. John and Teesha suggest that when the church fails to take a stand against racism, that failure could actually be a hindrance to some people coming to faith in Jesus Christ. Do you agree? Why?

4. While the church may be thriving in other parts of the world, it is losing ground in the United States. One partial explanation may be that the church has failed to provide moral leadership in areas like the fight against racism. Do you think this is true? Why?

Chapter Seventeen

FRIENDSHIP 101

When someone asked Abe Lincoln, after he was elected president, what he was going to do about his enemies, he replied, "I am going to destroy them. I am going to make them my friends."

—possible apocryphal tale that
John and Teesha really like

Some of you don't need a chapter on becoming friends with people who don't look like you. Your circle of friendship is already quite diverse. You already know the value of that diversity. If that's you, feel free to skim through this chapter or skip it entirely. But there are others of you out there whose friendships are limited to those who share your ethnicity. If that's you, then read on. We had you in mind when we wrote these ideas about friendship.

So, where to start? How about we start at the beginning by thinking about how friendships begin. You'll quickly realize that all friendships start by having a conversation with someone you don't know. You're at a party. You're at a church fellowship. You're at a freshman orientation. You're on a coffee break during a conference. Your friends are either occupied with someone else or not in attendance. Drink in hand, you decide to walk up to a stranger and start a conversation. For some of us, starting a conversation with a stranger is as easy as taking a bite of pizza. But for the introverts among us, talking to strangers is a big deal. So, this first conversation might not happen in a big crowd. It might happen quietly in the office break room where you cross paths with that new person who works three cubes over from you.

Regardless of the setting, regardless of your introversion or extraversion, every friendship starts with that first conversation. Not every conversation starts a friendship, but no friendship starts without one. That's just the way it works.

In this chapter we want to explore the idea of becoming friends with people who don't look like you. That idea is at the core of this book. And if all friendships start with a conversation, then the key to diversifying your friendships is getting used to the idea of talking to a more diverse group of people. If

> **Every friendship starts with that first conversation.**

you're black, it might mean starting to talk to white people. If you're Latino/Latina, it might mean starting to talk to Asian people. You get the point.

It's important, though, not to get ahead of yourself. Going to a party with the expectation that you're going to start a friendship with somebody will likely create a lot of pressure. What we're talking about here is much less daunting. Just go to the party and be open. Decide you're going to enjoy talking to whomever you bump into.

Maybe that'll be a black person. Maybe that'll be a white person. Just relax and have a good time. You might not talk about anything more substantial than the weather or your favorite sports team. But that's fine. The point is you had a pleasant conversation. And that's a start.

This may happen time and again. The conversation may never move past a few moments of enjoyable banter with someone you'll never see again. But when that enjoyable banter is with a person outside of your ethnic group, that's a win. You are slowly lowering the barrier between you and people who don't look like you and becoming acclimated to diversity.

Hopefully, someday that pleasant conversation is going to lead to another pleasant conversation . . . and another . . . and another. And you'll wake up one day and realize that person is no longer just a pleasant person to talk to; that person has become your friend. That's what we want to talk about for the rest of this chapter.

You can be intentional about having a conversation at a party with someone who doesn't look like you. It's solely about making a choice and having the social skills to pleasantly engage with someone for a few minutes. Friendship, however, is a different story.

Friendship is received, not taken. It's a gift, wrapped in interpersonal chemistry and common interests. It's framed by enjoyment, trust, and respect. It's fueled by communication. There are times when it will be hard work. But when it's getting started, it usually feels effortless. This is true whether your new friend looks like you or not.

So, what happens when that person you met at last year's Christmas party, who looks nothing like you, has become your friend? Our first response to that question is to caution you

Friendship is received, not taken.

about something. We have said this before, but it bears repeating. Austin Channing Brown, in her book *I'm Still Here: Black Dignity in a World Made for Whiteness*, begins by saying, "White people can be exhausting."[1] When asked about this in an interview, she replied, "The goal of our friendship shouldn't be for me to be your teacher. It should be me as your friend."[2] Her point is simple. If your new black friend starts to feel like you've made them your (unpaid) tutor on race relations, it's gonna wear them out. They want to be your friend not your consultant. Austin Channing Brown suggests that, rather than depending exclusively on your black friend to educate you, you should be reading and listening to all sorts of voices in order to understand what it's like to be black in the United States. But if you place that burden exclusively on the shoulders of your black friend, the spontaneity of friendship will be replaced with a stultifying sense of obligation.

As we mentioned earlier, there needs to be a sense of effortlessness to friendship. C. S. Lewis, in his book *The Four Loves*, says friends are people who aren't looking at each other but rather looking together at a shared interest, a shared love of something.[3] That's where friendship gets the energy that fuels the effortlessness. If you and I both love sports, movies, or food, it will not be hard to work up some energy to talk about those things. The energy is already there. We're just thrilled to find someone who loves the same things we do. Our friendship will be easy because it's fueled by the love of a common interest.

> *If your new black friend starts to feel like you've made them your (unpaid) tutor on race relations, it's gonna wear them out.*

This doesn't mean you'll never talk about anything else. It just means that you start with something that's energizing, not manufactured; something that you love to talk about, not something you think you should talk about. By the way, that dreary sense of obligation, often represented by the word *should*, kills friendships. So, if you can avoid "shoulding on yourself," as Brennan Manning used to say, and instead build up a backlog of enjoyable conversations over the weeks and months, you'll discover that something new is starting to grow between you. You are starting to trust one another.

Trust is confidence that someone is for you, that they want you to be happy. It's that conviction that they have your back; that, should the occasion ever arise, they will defend you against your critics. Trust is the assurance that they will tell you the truth not to hurt you but to help you. A friendship may start because of mutual interest, but it will last because of mutual trust.

Trust is the catalyst that allows a friendship to move beyond mutual interest into the realm of mutual discovery. It is the perception that it is safe to explore certain issues and ideas together. Not all friendships make it this far. Some friendships exist within certain boundaries. There is a tacit agreement that "We won't go there. We will stay where it's safe."

But there are other friendships where trust and curiosity carry the conversation beyond what's safe into those unknown areas where differences might live. Those differences are not necessarily disagreements. They're just the result of differing circumstances and experiences.

> *Trust is the catalyst that allows a friendship to move beyond mutual interest into the realm of mutual discovery.*

When you're friends with someone who doesn't look like you, it's this territory of the unknown that holds the greatest opportunity for life change. It's this territory where someone else's perspectives and experiences can shape your view of the world.

Of course, if I feel like my friend is trying to change me when I encounter these differences, I will probably retreat to the areas where it feels safe. But here's the thing—friends don't change one another because of an agenda. Friends change one another by allowing their friend to get close enough to see who they are, to see what they think and what they feel, and to understand why they think and feel that way. When my friend has the courage to tell me how her past has shaped her present perceptions, that's when her past will start to shape me as well. But the sharing is not done because she wants to change me. It's done because she wants me to know her. And when that person doesn't look like you, that knowledge can be transformative.

Here's a small example of what we're talking about. After we (Teesha and John) had been working together for a while, our conversations began to venture into some sensitive areas regarding racial issues. We took it one step at a time, slowly building up the trust between us. But each time one of us took a small risk, we were met with vulnerability and respect from the other. Nobody got attacked. Nobody got shamed. And there was never a sense that we were trying to change the other. We were trying to understand and be understood by the other. Here's a conversation we had early on in this process.

"So, I have a question for you."

"Now what?" said Teesha, rolling her eyes.

(Just kidding. Humor plays an integral role in our friendship.)

"Being from SoCal, sometimes I'm not sure how the race thing works here in the South."

"What do you mean?"

"Well, for example, sometimes I'm not sure what to call you guys."

I pointed out that in SoCal "guys" is a gender-neutral term. I quickly added that I was worried about offending people.

"So, should I refer to you as 'black' or 'African American' or what?"

"Well, technically, I'm not an African American, but I don't mind being referred to that way," said Teesha.

"What do you mean?"

"My family's from Jamaica. I'm Jamaican. If you use the term 'African American,' in a sense you're leaving me and my family out. It doesn't really account for my Jamaican heritage."

"So, it's black?"

"Well, that's the most inclusive term as it relates to my race. I'm black. So, yes, that's probably good most of the time. But some black people might prefer 'African American.' Black American can also be appropriate."

"Well, how am I gonna know what people prefer?"

"I suppose you'll have to ask them."

"As in we should actually talk about things like this rather than just make assumptions?"

"Exactly."

"Got it."

I learned something important about Teesha that day. She identifies as black rather than African American. Who knew? But I learned something else from that conversation as well. The truth is that no black person wants to represent their entire race. They are individuals. They are not icons that represent "their people." Such thinking, as Austin

> *The truth is that no black person wants to represent their entire race.*

Channing Brown mentioned, wears them out. It puts pressure on them, the kind of pressure that squelches friendships. But there's something else.

When I attempt to make Teesha a "stand-in for people of color everywhere" rather than becoming familiar with the black community around me, I take a step in the direction of tokenism, as in making only a token effort to understand black peoples' culture and experience. It's that thing where white people cultivate one relationship with one black person in order to create a veneer of diversity. It doesn't really matter who they are. I don't really need to know them. I just need to make sure people see me with them, see that we have "one of them" on our board, in our office, and so on so I can check the "I am okay with black people" box. Tokenism robs people of their humanity and turns them into symbols I am exploiting for my benefit. It is a subtle form of racism.

A person who senses that he is your token will never allow himself to become your friend. And real friends will never allow someone who doesn't look like them to become their "token." I learned all this by reflecting on a two-minute conversation with my friend Teesha. She wasn't trying to change me. She was just trying to let me know who she was. And yet, I was changed. Just a little bit. And only after thinking about the conversation. But it happened. That is the power of friendship.

> *A person who senses that he is your token will never allow himself to become your friend.*

As we mentioned earlier, this idea is the foundation upon which this book rests. By asking good questions, listening carefully to one another, and reflecting on what was said, we are not the same people we were five years ago. It hasn't always been a smooth ride. We have both said things there were offensive and needed an apology. We have both said things that were hard to hear, not because they were insensitive but because they were true. But these occasional difficulties fall on a cushion of trust and respect that has been built up over the years.

Let's sum this up. Friendship changes you. And when you change, your world changes. And when your world changes, *the* world changes. Maybe not much. Maybe not perfectly. But enough to make a tiny difference. And when enough people make a tiny difference, the cumulative effect is not tiny. Some people argue that real change always happens from the top down. That is not always true when we live in a healthy, functioning democracy. In his book *Democracy Matters*, Cornel West says, "The greatest intellectual, moral, political, and spiritual resources in America that may renew the soul and preserve the future of American democracy reside in this multi-racial, rich democratic heritage." West continues:

> But we must remember that the basis of democrat-
> ic leadership is ordinary citizens' desire to take their
> country back from the hands of corrupted plutocratic
> and imperial elites. . . . This is what happened in the
> 1860s, 1890s, 1930s, and 1960s in American history.
> Just as it looked as if we were about to lose the Ameri-
> can democratic experiment . . . in each of these periods
> a democratic awakening and activistic energy emerged
> to keep our democratic project afloat.[4]

We would suggest that sometimes the spirit of democracy flows through friendships. When those friendships exist between people from different ethnic groups, we have the best chance to participate in a society that values justice for everyone. It is in that sense that friendships can disrupt racism. But there's one more thing we want to mention.

It's tempting to see this emphasis on friendship as disconnected from the larger mission of the church. When we think of that mission, we tend to focus on issues of cultural relevance such as music, the message, and mission projects. These are very important, but they can't be the exclusive focus of our missional efforts. We think friendship is a crucial component in this area. Two thousand years ago, Jesus said, "By this all men will know you are my disciples . . ."

Friendship changes you. And when you change, your world changes. And when your world changes, the world changes.

He didn't complete the sentence with:

"...if you play the right music."
"...if you have a great communicator on stage."
"...if your website looks fresh and compelling."
"...if you're sending people on mission trips to the right countries."

He completed the sentence by saying: "... if you have love for one another" (John 13:35).

The word used here for love is *agape*, a Greek word that doesn't denote a feeling or affection. It denotes a particular stance toward the other. Jesus is talking about the fresh and fearless resolve to seek what is best "for one another."

Everyone will know you are my disciples if you have love for one another.

Everyone will know you are my disciples if you fearlessly pursue what is best, not for yourself, but for the other.

The implication is as unavoidable as it is clear. How we treat one another is tied to our effort to preach the gospel in that it identifies the ones who represent the gospel in the world.

So, take a minute. Who are the "one anothers" in your life? If they all look like you, we are, in effect, saying the gospel only works under a limited set of circumstances. As a result, we have taken something bigger than we can possibly conceive and shrunk it down to the size of our comfort zone. That makes God look smaller than God really is. And that, my friends, is not what Jesus had in mind.

DISCUSSION QUESTIONS

1. Does making friends come easily to you, or do you find it to be a significant challenge?

2. Is your circle of friends diverse, or is it pretty homogeneous? Do you feel like your circle of friends is fine the way it is, or are you starting to think about seeing it become more diverse?

3. Why do black people object when a white acquaintance leans too heavily on them to learn about racial issues?

4. What is tokenism? Do you think there's such a thing as "white tokenism," or is "tokenism" mainly a helpful way of examining how some white people treat black people?

5. John and Teesha suggest that when loving one another (as Jesus mentions in John 13:35) occurs only between people who look like each other, we have taken a big idea and shrunk it down to a size much smaller than Jesus intended. Do you agree?

Chapter Eighteen

NUDGING THE SYSTEM

Never doubt that a small group of thoughtful, committed citizens can change the world. Indeed, it is the only thing that ever has.

—*Margaret Mead*

If you pay even a tiny bit of attention to Hollywood, then you have probably heard of Jessica Chastain and Octavia Spencer. You may have seen Octavia Spencer in *Hidden Figures* or *The Shack* and Jessica Chastain in *Zero Dark Thirty* and the *Zookeeper's Wife*. They appeared together in *The Help*. Spencer is black; Chastain is white. During a panel at a recent Sundance Film Festival, Spencer shared a story of how Chastain had nudged the system.[1]

Chastain approached Spencer about a project she was producing. When they began discussing Spencer's pay, they agreed to address the disparity in pay between male and female actors. However, Spencer also raised the larger issue of race when she told Chastain that women of color earn far less than white women in the entertainment industry. Spencer was vulnerable. She put all of her cards on the table and disclosed the relevant figures. Chastain was stunned. She had no idea that this was the reality for women of color. Chastain knew that she had to act because "your silence is your discrimination." Chastain decided to tie her compensation to Spencer's so that they would equally divide a larger pot. It turns out that this resulted in Spencer being paid five times her normal salary. Spencer later described Chastain as both a listening friend and a vocal advocate.

Here you have two women, both actresses, both award-winning and critically acclaimed, both famous. But a difference between them is that one is black and one is white, a difference that turned out to have an economic impact. Chastain was first a friend as she listened to Spencer's experience. When she learned of the pay disparity along racial lines, she did not excuse it away. She did not conjure up any rationalizations about why she deserved more money than Spencer. She saw her friend for who she was, an immensely talented and experienced actress who should be appropriately compensated for her work regardless of her race. She saw an injustice. Once she saw it, she could not unsee it. She had to act. For Chastain, silence was synonymous with complicity, which she could not countenance. Chastain's friendship compelled her to nudge the system.

We have talked a lot about the importance of entering into relationships with people who don't look like you. It is an essential step in disrupting racism and living out the gospel. But it is just the first step. Friendship is a foundation for the concrete work of reforming systems and institutions infected with racism. Loving someone who doesn't look like you will make you see the world differently. Once you see injustice, you cannot unsee it. Love demands that we seek to end the present harm being inflicted on our brothers and sisters of color and prevent future harm from coming to them.

Consider your sibling or a childhood friend. If someone was bullying them and it was within your power to stop it, would you be justified in doing nothing? Probably not. You would stand up to the bully on behalf of your sibling or childhood friend. There would likely be broad agreement that this is the right and moral thing to do. Likewise, if someone gave your brother or sister an underinflated football that wouldn't travel as far or as fast

> *Friendship is a foundation for the concrete work of reforming systems and institutions infected with racism.*

at the start of a game, placing them on unequal footing as compared to those on the other team, would you remain silent? Probably not. We predict that you would be pretty upset that someone had treated your sibling so unfairly. It would not take much to convince you that you should step in on behalf of your sibling and do whatever is within your power to ensure that the game is played fairly. This same sense of familial love and responsibility should characterize your relationships with one another, even and especially those who are different from you. If you take seriously the notion that we are brothers and sisters in Christ, then neither inaction nor silence is an acceptable response to racial injustice. Having established a necessary foundation of friendship, the next step is to nudge the system by taking concrete steps to move the country, in large and small ways, toward racial equality.

The first step is to pray. We've said this before. It's easy to skip this step. You may be more concerned about getting the work done, especially if you are a task-oriented person who loves to-do lists. You want to do something real and concrete to address the pain that you continue to observe. There is a lot of work to be done, and you are not wrong for wanting to get started. However, it is important that the work of nudging the system be done through God and for God's glory. Bringing light to the dark places of racist institutions and communities suffering under the consequences of those institutions is God's work, but we get to play a part. That's where prayer comes in: pray for racial justice, pray for wisdom and guidance, pray for direction in the work, and above all, pray the words of Isaiah in response to the Lord's question about whom to send to proclaim the Lord's message: "'Here am I! Send me.'" (Isaiah 6:8).

After engaging the simple but essential first step of placing God squarely at the center of your work through prayer, you can begin to take stock of your spheres of influence. Jessica Chastain is an actress who has a certain amount of power and influence in the film industry. What are the spaces and places in which you have power and influence? Notice, we did not say "the places where you are in charge." So many of us fall into the trap of thinking that we need a title, money, or fame to lead or effect change. That could not be further from the truth. Scripture is full of stories of God using unlikely people to bring about God's purposes, like Abraham, Mary the mother of Jesus, David, Rahab, and Tamar. We all have the capacity to do good for our neighbor. Proverbs 3:27-28 says, "Do not withhold good from those to whom it is due, when it is in your power to do it. Do not say to your neighbor, 'Go, and come again, tomorrow I will give it'—when you have it with you." The focus is on the ability to give goodness to our neighbor, not on titles or wealth.

Our spheres of influence are the places where we have power to do good, to give goodness, on behalf of our neighbor. These are the places you frequent and the people whom you know and who know you. We all have places where there are opportunities to be a catalyst for change. You need only spend a bit of time reviewing your life in order to identify them. As you take stock of your spheres of influence, consider writing them down. This simple act makes the idea that you have power and influence to effect change on issues of race more concrete and tangible. A few obvious places of influence are your workplace, church, and small group. Add these to your list. But be creative in your thinking. Where do you spend time? Who are your friends and where do they gather? What about your children's school, your softball team, your running club, your book club, your fantasy football league, your neighborhood, or your city? What about your own family? Others of you may have some political influence. You might sense a calling to hop on a plane to work on racial justice at a national level. If that's you, we love that! However, most of us are rooted in particular communities, families, and workplaces. What are the places where you have influence right now, right where you are? That you do not have influence in every space or in seemingly big ways should not be a source of disillusionment. You have influence in some spaces, which means you have the potential to have an impact. Don't forget that many small impacts, when combined, can lead to real, lasting, and substantial change.

Once you've taken stock of the spaces in which you have influence, observe and investigate the racial dynamics in those spaces. When Jessica Chastain began paying attention, she discovered (through her friendship with Octavia Spencer) that black actresses were paid less than their white counterparts. Be aware and be curious about how racism is playing out in your spaces of influence. Who is present? Who seems to be absent? What might account for these observations?

Let's take the school in your community for example. As you seek greater awareness of the racial dynamics in your spheres of influence, you might ask about the racial makeup of the students, teachers, administrators, and the school board. How do these figures compare with schools in nearby communities? How do these schools compare in other ways, like in their after-school programs, extracurricular activities, availability of technology, age and quality of textbooks, availability of music and art classes, and so on? Then you might ask why these institutions look and function the way they do and how they are funded. Answering these questions may require you to speak with the principal, a member of the school board, or your child's teacher. You may also have to do some internet research and check out a few books at your local library. You may decide to seek out some relevant podcasts or documentaries as well. Learning about how racial dynamics currently function and have functioned in the past are important precursors to any effort to impact change in the system. Focusing your learning in the areas where you have influence brings the reality of racism a little closer to home. It may be difficult, but it can be empowering. As you learn, you are gathering tools that will allow you to tangibly improve the problems you discover.

Ideally, each step of this process will be bathed in prayer as you continually give this work over to God. As Christians, our faith informs all of life. It extends far beyond Sunday morning and includes the work of justice. The world needs an activism rooted in the gospel and driven by the Holy Spirit. Ask how God might be leading you to engage in some of the problems you have identified. As you pray, consider what Scriptures and traditions speak to the issues you found. For example, if you have been looking at racial dynamics in a school in your neighborhood, what does the Bible have to say about children? How did Jesus treat children? Do the policies and procedures of your school oppose Scripture's view of children? You might also think about identifying people who are already engaged in the work of bringing about racial justice in the spheres you have been researching. Maybe God is leading you to join them in their work.

We have laid out several steps in the process of engaging the work of transforming systems of injustice. However, these don't have to be discrete, linear steps. You will likely move back and forth among these steps multiple times, but the important thing to remember is to intentionally engage each step.

Wherever your prayer and research lead you, we hope it is toward action. Thoughts and prayers matter. They are an important part of the work of undoing the inequities that centuries of racist policies have created. The work begins with thoughts and prayers, but it cannot end there. It is time for Christians to roll up their sleeves and decide that enough is enough. It is time to do the work that the gospel requires of us.

A word of encouragement is probably in order. You may cycle through many emotions while working for justice. There will be days when you feel discouraged. Doing the work of justice can be emotionally exhausting. While doing this work, you will be further exposed to how deeply and widely people of color have been impacted by racism in America. It is likely that what you see and hear might cause anger or discouragement. In those moments, remember the suffering of the people you're trying to serve. Then don't give up.

It is time for Christians to roll up their sleeves and decide that enough is enough. It is time to do the work that the gospel requires of us.

DISCUSSION QUESTIONS

1. What does nudging the system mean? How did actress Jessica Chastain nudge the system?

2. Do you agree with the underlying assumption of this chapter—that if enough people nudge the system, the system will change?

3. Are you in a place where you might be willing to consider nudging the system? If so, what system are you thinking about nudging?

4. Is nudging the system inherently risky? What kinds of risks might be encountered? How does God figure into your thinking about taking such risks?

Chapter Nineteen

HOW LONG?

It isn't that the evil thing wins—it never will—but that it doesn't die.

—*John Steinbeck*

There are a lot of books on racial justice and reconciliation out there. One of our favorites is *The Children* by David Halberstam. It is a history of the civil rights movement. Halberstam tells this story by weaving together the stories of the fifteen or twenty men and women who were at the center of it all. While Martin Luther King Jr. is frequently mentioned, Halberstam focuses on other, less famous men and women who played a central role in the fight for civil rights. (They were all so young that an early advocate for the movement called them "children" even though they were in their twenties.)

We don't often hear the names of these less famous activists: Jim Lawson. Diane Nash. Bernard Lafayette. C. T. Vivian. James Bevel.

Gloria Johnson. Curtis Murphy. Rodney Powell. God used these "children" to shape and give direction to one of the most important movements in American history.

Halfway through the book, Halberstam includes several pages of black-and-white photographs. John spent time with these pictures, getting familiar with the faces behind the stories. It's an interesting assortment. There are typical family photos scattered among photos of historical significance. For example, on one page there's a picture of Jim Lawson being arrested on the steps of the First Baptist Church in Nashville, Tennessee, in 1961. Right next to it, there's a photo of John Lewis and his wife, Lillian, on their wedding day. It's a reminder that these men and women are a lot like us. They're not one-dimensional ideologues. They're people who married (or didn't), liked to read (or didn't), enjoyed hiking (or opera, or football). They did the same things that all the rest of us do. But woven into those normal activities were some things that changed the history of our country.

One of the most poignant examples of this is the portrayal of Bernard Lafayette. On one page, we see ten-year-old Bernard Lafayette all dressed up for Sunday school, circa 1950. One page later, there's another picture of twenty-one-year-old Bernard Lafayette with little hills of bloody flesh poking through his close-cropped hair. They were the points of impact between his skull and the night sticks of the state troopers who decided he shouldn't be causing trouble in their "peaceful" town. Turn the page one more time and you see a middle-aged Bernard Lafayette, standing with his wife, Kate, twenty years after the movement ended.

If you turn the page again, there's a picture of people marching across Pettus Bridge in Selma, Alabama, on what came to be known as "Bloody Sunday." Framed in the picture are a group of blue-helmeted police, watching the procession. Just moments after that picture was snapped, they turned on the crowd and began to beat them with clubs. There's a picture of John Lewis on the ground that day, surrounded by the men in the blue helmets. He was in the middle of being beaten half to death.

All those people. All that pain. All those accomplishments. The physical courage they evidenced time and time again as they marched into the jaws of the battle. The spiritual resolve they exemplified as they refused to meet violence with violence. It's unforgettable.

Those young men and women pictured in Halberstam's book are old now. Some went on to lead lives of public service after the civil rights era. One or two burnt down their lives with one bad decision after another. But most slipped back into obscurity along with the rest of us, a bright burst of light and life that flamed up and then disappeared. Thank God for books like Halberstam's that give us a way to remember their sacrifice and celebrate their lives.

So where do things stand now? Fifty years after the civil rights movement, there are laws on the books that make some forms of racism illegal. Sports teams, universities, and the armed services are diverse in a way that would have been unimaginable two generations ago. But the victories are incomplete. They occur in a wider cultural context where hate crimes against people of color are still fairly common. Black people still have less money and more jail time than white people, facts that are inexplicable apart from conceding that either the racists are right or that the poison they've injected into our society is still active.

How long is this going to go on? The fight against racism in our country is more than four hundred years old. We've made some progress, but there's a long road ahead. How can we continue to fight this ongoing battle without being consumed by it? How do we avoid becoming like the ones whom we oppose, bitter and angry, refusing to see the image of God that exists in the people they hate? These are crucial questions. There are answers, but they aren't simple. They require some explanation.

For starters, it's important to affirm that in one sense the battle against evil, including racist evil, has already been won. In Jesus Christ, the kingdom of God has already invaded this world. As we mentioned earlier, the first thing Jesus said on the day He started His public ministry was, "'Repent, for the kingdom of heaven is at hand'" (Matthew 4:17). And when Jesus died on the cross, the evil power that previously ruled the world was defeated.

> *There's a long road ahead. How can we continue to fight this ongoing battle without being consumed by it?*

There is, says the apostle Paul, now no condemnation for those who are in Christ Jesus (Romans 8:1). In Galatians, Paul says, "There is neither Jew nor Greek, there is neither slave nor free, there is neither male nor female; for you are all one in Christ Jesus" (Galatians 3:28). It is, as Jesus said on the cross, finished. The work has been completed.

There is a big "however" here. While it is true that the war against evil has been won in Jesus Christ, the battles between good and evil continue to rage. We fight as those who have hope, but still we fight. The victory has been won by Jesus, but that victory is not yet final.

Christians love to talk about "already but not yet," but that kind of thinking isn't limited to theological matters. Military historians tell us that, strategically speaking, the European theater of WWII was won on D-Day, June 6, 1944, when the Allies (Britain, Canada, and the United States) invaded the beaches of Normandy. Yet the victory wasn't finalized until eleven months later on May 8, 1945, when Germany surrendered. Between the defeat and the surrender of Nazi Germany, there was almost a year of costly, difficult battle where thousands of soldiers sacrificed their lives. So, while the war against evil has been won on the cross of Jesus Christ and that victory validated by His resurrection, we are still fighting until the enemy surrenders. Already but not yet. It's the tension in which we live.

The thing is, we don't know how much longer these battles will rage. And there is some debate among Christians as to whether things will get better or worse before Jesus returns, finalizing the victory He won on the cross. So, what do we do in the meantime? How do we "fight the good fight" without losing hope? How do we look evil in the eye without letting that vision crush us?

> *We fight as those who have hope, but still we fight.*

How do we avoid bitterness and despair when we know that however today's battle went, there will be more tomorrow?

The apostle Paul provides an example here. Talk about wrestling with evil! In 2 Corinthians 11:24-27, he gives us a list of all that he has suffered:

> Five times I have received at the hands of the Jews the forty lashes less one. Three times I have been beaten with rods; once I was stoned. Three times I have been shipwrecked; a night and a day I have been adrift at sea; on frequent journeys, in danger from rivers, danger from robbers, danger from my own people, danger from Gentiles, danger in the city, danger in the wilderness, danger at sea, danger from false brethren; in toil and hardships, through many a sleepless night, in hunger and thirst, often without food, in cold and exposure.

The amount of suffering Paul endured is staggering. And on top of it all, what he didn't know when he catalogued these events, was that eventually he would be put in prison and executed by the Roman government . . . simply for following Jesus.

The only thing more staggering than Paul's suffering is the hope and joy he experienced in the midst of it all. In Romans 8:18, Paul says, "I consider the suffering of this present time is not worth comparing with the glory that is to be revealed to us." In Ephesians 2:7 he writes about the immeasurable riches of God's grace. Later in that letter he continues:

> and that Christ may dwell in your hearts through faith;
> that you, being rooted and grounded in love, may have
> power to comprehend with all the saints what is the
> breadth and length and height and depth, and to know
> the love of Christ which surpasses knowledge, that you
> may be filled with all the fulness of God. (3:17-19)

The point is this. Paul maintained hope in the face of despair, joy amid suffering, and love in the midst of circumstances that should have twisted his soul into a bitter, fearful mess. He did this by maintaining an unwavering focus on what God has done in Jesus Christ. But this was more than just a focus on ideas and events. Paul experienced the presence of Jesus with him. The work Jesus did was given emotional power in Paul's life by the intimacy of Jesus's presence. We can sum this up by saying that attempting to fight evil for Jesus, apart from an intimate connection with Jesus, will result in losing the hope offered us by Jesus. So, as we strive to disrupt racism one friendship at a time, it is crucial that we encourage our friends to follow Paul's example. We must not try to advance the work of the kingdom apart from being with the King. Otherwise, our days will be dreary. Our nights will be full of despair. And we just won't last very long in the battle against the great evil of racism.

It's beyond the scope of this book to give a detailed account of how to cultivate this intimacy with God. If you feel like you need a little coaching in this area, pick up a copy of *Emotionally Healthy Spirituality* by Peter Scazzero. In that book, Scazzero gives a comprehensive overview of how to cultivate a life-giving relationship with Jesus even during the most demanding situations.

You also might want to read *Under the Unpredictable Plant* by Eugene H. Peterson.[1] It's a study of the life of Jonah. You will quickly see the many parallels there are between Jonah's work of calling Nineveh to repentance and our work of calling our country to repent of racism. There is one line from Peterson's book that is profoundly disturbing. Reflecting on the quality of Jonah's life, Peterson says, "But Jonah is worse obedient than he was disobedient." Peterson here is not referring to Jonah's famous attempt to flee from God's presence. He is referring to the hate Jonah has for Nineveh as he is obediently following God's directives to preach to them. Peterson points out that "Jonah obeys to the letter the command of God, but Jonah betrays the spirit of God with his anger."[2]

Pursuing racial justice apart from being shaped and formed by God's loving presence makes us vulnerable to the hate and fear that characterized Jonah's obedience and that so often surrounds the conversation about race in the United States. It is only by paying careful attention to our souls, as Paul did and as Peterson counsels us to do, that we will avoid being a casualty of the battles we fight. Ironically, the possibility of becoming weary, bitter, and angry by neglecting our spiritual health is a much more prevalent danger than whatever wounds we might receive at the hands of the racists God calls us to lovingly oppose.

This is all the more important because, as we said earlier, we have no idea how long these battles are going to last. The most information the disciples could pry out of Jesus was that His second coming would be a surprise and that even He didn't know exactly when it would happen (Matthew 24:36). So we must acquire a vision that will not grow faint with age.

Martin Luther King Jr. had such a vision. Nowhere is it stated more clearly and compellingly than during his famous "I Have a Dream" speech given on the steps of the Lincoln Memorial on August 28, 1963. In the course of that speech, he said:

> I say to you today, my friends, though, even though we face the difficulties of today and tomorrow, I still have a dream. It is a dream deeply rooted in the American dream. I have a dream that one day this nation will rise up, live out the true meaning of its creed: "We hold these truths to be self-evident, that all men are created equal."
>
> I have a dream that one day on the red hills of Georgia sons of former slaves and the sons of former slave-owners will be able to sit down together at the table of brotherhood. I have a dream that one day even the state of Mississippi, a state sweltering with the heat of injustice, sweltering with the heat of oppression, will be transformed into an oasis of freedom and justice.
>
> I have a dream that my four little children will one day live in a nation where they will not be judged by the color of their skin but by the content of their character. I have a dream . . .

Clearly, we have made some progress since the days of the civil rights movement. The sons and daughters of former slaves and slaveholders are sitting down together. In town after town, in school after school, in neighborhood after neighborhood, the pain of racial injustice has been replaced by the pleasure of living together in freedom. All across the country, people of all colors are increasingly being judged by their character rather than their color. This is already happening, but it is not yet happening everywhere.

Today a black woman will be on the receiving end of a racist insult lobbed at her by a white coworker. Today a black man will sit on the side of the road being interrogated by two white state troopers who pulled him over because he looked more suspicious than his white counterparts. Today a black home buyer will be denied a

This is already happening, but it is not yet happening everywhere.

loan to buy a home in a desirable neighborhood because the realtor doesn't want to adversely affect property values. And today a black inmate will be beaten by a white prison gang with swastikas tattooed on their arms.

Already but not yet. We have won, but we haven't yet obtained the final victory against evil. As John Steinbeck said in the quote at the beginning of this chapter, "It isn't that the evil thing wins—it never will—but that it doesn't die."

So how do we proceed? How do we move forward while we live in this tension between already and not yet? The answer is as encouraging as it is practical. We move forward one day, one act at a time. Pastor Andy Stanley helps us lean into this idea more deeply when he says, "Do for one what you can't do for all." It's brilliant advice. We cannot encourage everyone, but we can encourage someone. We can't befriend everyone, but we can become friends with someone.

The guy next door. The family down the street. The gal in the cubicle next to ours. That new lady in our tennis club. The person walking her dog in our neighborhood. One at a time. The person who doesn't look like you. Maybe we can't change the world, but we can change our world, disrupting racism one friendship at a time.

Perhaps you feel like this one-at-a-time approach is a "runner-up" option, something we have to settle for because we can't figure out how to do better. That is not true because it leaves God out of the equation. It turns out that God is incredibly efficient. God wastes nothing. He can take the one thing you did and combine it with the one thing somebody else did. Then God will take that pair of actions and combine it with a few things that some other people did. Suddenly, what seemed to be isolated acts of kindness are being knit together to generate momentum and impact. Under God's skilled direction, movements are slowly being born, fueled by God's sovereign hand.

Jim Lawson, one of the "children" David Halberstam mentioned, talks about the vision of a beloved kingdom. God is building that kingdom as we speak, and He is doing it through you. We are participating in something much bigger than us. "Doing for one" represents the building blocks that God uses to accomplish God's purpose in the world.

> *"Doing for one" represents the building blocks that God uses to accomplish God's purpose in the world.*

Think of it. We will never act to prevent suffering but that God will not leverage our effort. We will never restore dignity to someone created in God's image but that God will leverage that restoration a hundred times over. We will never refuse to hate but that God will take our refusal and use it to staunch the flow of hatred in the world. We will never laugh together but that God will cause our laughter to dispel sadness. And we will never cry together but that God will sew peace and freedom with the seed of our tears.

This is what our infinite God will do through us. We will sometimes stumble and fall. Sometimes evil will carry the day. Sometimes we will lose a battle. But the war has been won. The kingdom of God is never in trouble. Jesus may return because things have become unbearably bad. He may return because things have become unbearably good. Who knows? Either way, in the meantime, He will be building His kingdom. Racism, along with every other kind of evil, will be disrupted. And someday there will be no more tension between already and not yet, for the victory will be complete. And the friendships we built with people who don't look like us (and the people who do) will turn out to have been the firstfruits of a new reality. It will be better than we could have imagined. That's the end game. That's what disrupting racism, one friendship at a time, is all about.

And when this happens, when we allow freedom ring, when we let it ring from every village and every hamlet, from every state and every city, we will be able to speed up that day when all of God's children, black men and white men, Jews and Gentiles, Protestants and Catholics, will be able to join hands and sing in the words of the old Negro spiritual, "Free at last! Free at last! Thank God Almighty, we are free at last!"[3]

DISCUSSION QUESTIONS

1. How does your vision for your own activism change when you remember that most of the leaders of the civil rights movement were just normal people who were youngsters, grew up, got married, sometimes got divorced, and (eventually) had regular jobs?

2. Given that the civil rights movement occurred more than fifty years ago, how do you assess the progress we've made since then? In what ways have we made a lot of progress? In what ways have we made far too little?

3. When it comes to the future, are you hopeful about race relations in the United States? Why or why not?

4. How does your thinking change when you realize that God wants to use your choices and friendships to disrupt racism?

5. Thank you for reading this book! We hope it has been engaging and helpful. What next step are you thinking about as you consider how you might allow God to use you to continue to disrupt racism?

A TOOL KIT FOR ACTIVISTS

To Keep Them Centered, Strong, Effective, and Spiritually Whole

The following is an annotated list of books to help those involved in the fight against racism who also happen to be followers of Jesus. The list covers a variety of topics, from taking care of your soul to the strategic task of leading institutional change. The books are presented in alphabetical order by the author's last name. There are sections for Nonfiction, Fiction, and Creative Nonfiction. This "tool kit" is in no way comprehensive. Nevertheless, we hope it will be helpful.

NONFICTION

Bonhoeffer, Dietrich. *Life Together*. New York: HarperOne, 2009.
    Don't let the brevity of this book fool you. It is a profound
    treatment of community, written by Bonhoeffer when he

was inside Nazi Germany, on the run from the Gestapo
during WWII. His point is unmissable—serving Jesus
in any capacity must only be done in the context of
community.

Brother Lawrence. *The Practice of the Presence of God*. Independently
published, 2013.
Contrary to what you might think, this eighteenth-century
classic was written by a dishwasher in a monastery. His
point is that there's no reason to limit our intimate contact
with God to our quiet times of prayer and reading Scripture.

Brueggemann, Walter. *The Psalms and the Life of Faith*. Minneapolis:
Fortress, 1995.
This is essential reading for anyone who wants to be
sustained by the emotional and theological riches contained
in the Book of Psalms.

Buckingham, Marcus, and Donald Clifton. *Now, Discover Your
Strengths*. Washington, DC: Gallup, 2001.
Knowing yourself is essential whatever it is that you do with
your life. This book will help move that ball down the field.

Claiborne, Shane, Jonathan Wilson-Hartgrove, and Enuma Okoro.
Common Prayer: A Liturgy for Ordinary Radicals. Grand Rapids,
MI: Zondervan, 2010.
For hundreds of years, Christians have kept regular rhythms
of prayer in the morning and evening. This prayer book
combines modern and ancient practices and language to
deepen readers' experience of prayer, particularly around
issues of justice.

Foster, Richard, and James Bryan Smith, eds. *Devotional Classics.*
New York: HarperOne, 2005.

> This powerful collection of excerpts provides an
> introduction to the life and work of some of the great
> saints of the Christian faith, many of whom will be new to
> our readers. The editors take us on a far-reaching journey,
> connecting us with the likes of Thomas à Kempis and Teresa
> of Avila. There is even a brief introduction to C. S. Lewis.

Friedman, Edwin. *A Failure of Nerve.* New York: Church Publishing,
2017.

> Friedman contends that in the era of the quick fix (which
> tactic he debunks) it is the leader who has the courage to be
> himself who will produce the most important results.

Gutiérrez, Gustavo. *We Drink from Our Own Wells: The Spiritual
Journey of a People.* Maryknoll, NY: Orbis, 2003.

> A well-known liberation theologian, Gutiérrez explores
> the contours of the Christian life from a Latin American
> perspective, one that is rooted in a struggle for dignity and
> for life itself.

Hayes, Diana L. *Forged in the Fiery Furnace: African American
Spirituality.* Maryknoll, NY: Orbis, 2012.

> Hayes looks at how African Americans have lived out their
> faith in the "fiery furnace" of slavery, segregation, and
> present-day discrimination.

Holmes, Barbara A. *Joy Unspeakable: Contemplative Practices of the
Black Church.* Minneapolis: Fortress, 2017.

> We often think of contemplative practices as being part of

the Catholic tradition, but Holmes shows how communal contemplative practices have been part of the Protestant wing of the historic black church in America.

Johnson, Darrell W. *Experiencing the Trinity*. Vancouver, BC, Canada: Regent College Publishing, 2002.
> Rev. Johnson explores the idea that at the center of the universe there is a community in which we can participate.

Kotter, John. *Leading Change*. Brighton, MA: Harvard Business Review Press, 2012.
> John Kotter is one of the illuminati of the Harvard Business School. The book is not faith-based, but Kotter's experience with more than three hundred corporations provides a textbook for how to lead institutional change from the inside—a position activists often overlook.

MacKenzie, Gordon. *Orbiting the Giant Hairball*. New York: Viking, 1998.
> While this book is not written from a Christian perspective, it talks about a crucial question for Christian activists: How do we stay close to the institutions we hope to influence without being engulfed by them?

Nouwen, Henri J. M. *The Wounded Healer*. New York: Image, 1979.
> Pain is a part of every human life. Nouwen helps us to avoid the myriad of ways this can be mishandled. In so doing, he shows how pain can be used by God to make us whole and shape us in a way that will help us assist others deal with their pain.

Pressfield, Steven. *The War of Art*. Independently published, 2012.
    While Pressfield addresses the struggle writers and artists
    face, his point is eminently relevant to activists: the largest
    source of resistance you will likely have to overcome is not
    "the man." It's you. This book is definitely not written from a
    Christian perspective. *Language warning.*

Smedes, Lewis. *Forgive and Forget*. New York: HarperOne, 2007.
    If we don't master the art that Smedes writes about here, we
    will discover that the racist hate we face as activists will turn
    us into racist haters, ultimately no different than the people
    we oppose.

Thurman, Howard. *Disciplines of the Spirit*. Richmond, IN: Friends
    United Press, 1963.
    Pastor, educator, and theologian, Thurman explores five
    dimensions of the spiritual life—commitment, growing in
    wisdom and stature, suffering, prayer, and reconciliation.

FICTION

We are big believers in the idea that reading literature, nourishing the imagination, is an important part of the Christian life, the activist life, the well-lived human life. Beware: these books will sometimes make you angry, sometimes make you sad, sometimes cause offense, and sometimes make you glad to be playing a part in the fight against racism.

Adichie, Chimamanda Ngozi. *Americanah*. Norwell, MA: Anchor,
    2014.
Ellison, Ralph. *Invisible Man*. New York: Vintage, 1995.

Grisham, John. *A Time to Kill*. New York: Dell, 2009.

Hurston, Zora Neale. *Their Eyes Were Watching God*. New York: Harper Perennial Modern Classics, 2006.

Jordan, Hillary. *Mudbound*. Chapel Hill, NC: Algonquin, 2009.

Kidd, Sue Monk. *The Secret Life of Bees*. New York: Penguin, 2003.

Lee, Harper. *To Kill a Mockingbird*. New York: Harper Perennial Modern Classics, 2002.

Stockett, Kathryn. *The Help*. New York: Berkley, 2011.

Twain, Mark. *The Adventures of Huckleberry Finn*. Mineola, NY: Dover, 1994.

Walker, Alice. *The Color Purple*. Boston: Houghton Mifflin Harcourt, 1992.

CREATIVE NONFICTION

Shetterly, Margot Lee. *Hidden Figures*. New York: William Morrow, 2016.

Skloot, Rebecca. *The Immortal Life of Henrietta Lacks*. New York: Broadway Books, 2011.

NOTES

1. The Clock Is Ticking

1.   This is a reference to the February 8, 2017, shooting of Chad Robertson, an unarmed twenty-five-year-old black man who was fleeing on foot from the police.

2.   Samantha Raphelson, "Called to Rise: Dallas Police Chief on Overcoming Racial Division," National Public Radio, accessed September 10, 2018, www.npr.org/2017/06/06/531787065/called-to -rise-dallas-police-chief-on-overcoming-racial-division.

3.   Raphelson, "Called to Rise."

4.   Bob Zaltsberg, "How Can You Hate Me When You Don't Even Know Me?" *The Republic*, accessed September 10, 2018, www. therepublic.com/2018/09/09/how_can_you_hate_me_when_you_dont _even_know_me/.

3. I Once Was Blind but Now I'm Just Kinda Nearsighted

1.   I am telling my story here—those things that I remember and experienced. Had I been telling the story of baseball, I would have mentioned Jackie Robinson, the man who broke the color barrier in the major leagues. Initially, he was *not* cheered on the field. But that happened before I was born, so I've not included it in this chapter. Suffice it to say that the black athletes mentioned here were standing on his shoulders.

2. John Perkins, *Let Justice Roll Down* (Grand Rapids, MI: Baker, 2012).

4. You've Got to Be Kidding

1. The fact of an all-white jury shows that Emmett Till's murder is not reducible to "personal" racism. It was inseparable from the structural racism we discuss in the next chapter—structural racism that, in this case, made an all-white jury a given.

2. "2016 Hate Crime Statistics," Federal Bureau of Investigation Uniform Crime Reporting Program, accessed September 11, 2018, www.fbi.gov/news/stories/2016-hate-crime-statistics.

3. We chose to leave this word in the story without writing it out, because while we don't want to normalize its use neither do we want to remove the insult it carries.

5. Racism Isn't Always in Your Heart

1. During World War I, the federal government developed housing for nonmilitary personnel who were involved in the manufacturing of materials for use in fighting the war. See Richard Rothstein, *The Color of Law: A Forgotten History of How Our Government Segregated America* (New York: Liveright, 2017), 18–19.

2. Rothstein, *Color of Law*, xiv, 18–19, 20–30, 31–32.

3. Rothstein, 34, 180.

4. Rothstein, 63–64, 93–99.

5. Rothstein, 66.

6. There are several online resources where you can view the redlining maps created by the HOLC for neighborhoods across the United States. One such resource is *Mapping Inequality*, created by the University of Richmond (https://dsl.richmond.edu).

7. Emily Badger, "This Can't Happen by Accident," *Washington Post*,

May 2, 2016, www.washingtonpost.com/graphics/business/wonk
/housing/atlanta/.

8. Badger, "This Can't Happen by Accident."

9. Rothstein, *Color of Law*, 184.

10. Emily Badger et al., "Extensive Data Shows Punishing Reach of
Racism for Black Boys," *New York Times*, March 19, 2018, www.nytimes
.com/interactive/2018/03/19/upshot/race-class-white-and-black-men
.html.

11. Badger et al., "Extensive Data Shows Punishing Reach."

12. Rothstein, *Color of Law*, 178–79.

13. Joe R. Feagin and Bernice McNair Barnett, "Success and Failure:
How Systemic Racism Trumped the Brown v. Board of Education
Decision," *University of Illinois Law Review* 2004, no. 5 (2004): 1110–11.

14. Feagin and Barnett, "Success and Failure," 1110–13.

15. Feagin and Barnett, 1100.

16. Susan Egerter et al., "Issue Brief #5: Exploring the Social Detriments
of Health," Robert Wood Johnson Foundation, April 2011, accessed
November 11, 2018, www.rwjf.org/content/dam/farm/reports/issue
_briefs/2011/rwjf70447.

17. Michelle Alexander, *The New Jim Crow: Mass Incarceration in the
Age of Colorblindness* (New York: New Press, 2010), 5–6, 59.

18. Ashley Nellis, "The Color of Justice: Racial and Ethnic Disparities in
State Prisons," The Sentencing Project, June 14, 2016, www
.sentencingproject.org/publications/color-of-justice-racial-and-ethnic
-disparity-in-state-prisons/.

19. Alexander, *New Jim Crow*, 6.

20. Alexander, 7.

21. Douglas Stuart, *Hosea-Jonah*, Word Biblical Commentary 31 (Waco,
TX: Word, 1987), 316–17.

22. Stuart, *Hosea-Jonah*, 306.

23. Peggy McIntosh, "White Privilege: Unpacking the Invisible Knapsack," in Race, Class, and Gender in the United States: An Integrated Study, 9th ed., ed. Paula S. Rothenberg and Kelly S. Mayhew (New York: Worth, 2014), 175.

24. McIntosh, "White Privilege," 179.

25. McIntosh, 176.

7. White Fear

1. The Tuskegee Institute has documented the lynching of 1,297 white people between 1882 and 1968. These lynchings, however, were seldom if ever racially motivated.

2 Desmond Tutu, *No Future Without Forgiveness* (New York: Doubleday, 1999), 281.

8. Anger

1 Lytta Basset, *Holy Anger: Jacob, Job, and Jesus* (London: Continuum, 2007), 217.

2. Robin DiAngelo, "White Fragility," *International Journal of Critical Pedagogy* 3, no. 3 (2011): 57. See also Robin DiAngelo, *White Fragility: Why It's So Hard for White People to Talk about Racism* (Boston: Beacon, 2018).

9. What Holds Racism in Place?

1. C. S. Lewis, *Mere Christianity* (New York: Macmillan, 1960), 51.

2. W. H. Lewis, ed. *Letters of C. S. Lewis* (London: Geoffrey Bles, 1966), 261.

3. J. R. R. Tolkien, *The Hobbit* (New York: Ballantine, 1970), 196.

4. David Halberstam, *The Children* (New York: Fawcett, 1998), 441.

5. Lesslie Newbigin, *The Gospel in a Pluralist Society* (Grand Rapids: Eerdmans, 1989), 201.

6. Newbigin, *Gospel in a Pluralist Society.*

7. Newbigin, 204.

8. Newbigin, 210.

10. Fess Up

1. For an excellent overview of the theology and practice of lament, see Walter Brueggemann, "The Psalms as Prayer and Praise," part 1 in *The Psalms and the Life of Faith* (Minneapolis: Fortress, 1995). Our thinking here is indebted to his work in this area.

2. For an exhaustive study of the word *repent*, see Gerhard Kittel, ed., *The Theological Dictionary of the New Testament*, vol. 4, trans. Geoffrey Bromiley (Grand Rapids: Eerdmans, 1976), 1001–3.

3. Martin Luther King Jr., "Address at the Fourth Annual Institute on Nonviolence and Social Change at Bethel Baptist Church," Stanford University, The Martin Luther King Jr. Research and Education Institute, accessed September 14, 2018, https://kinginstitute.stanford.edu/king-papers/documents/address-fourth-annual-institute-nonviolence-and-social-change-bethel-baptist-0.

11. Specks and Planks

1. As we mentioned in chapter 7, Desmond Tutu in his book *No Future Without Forgiveness*, makes it clear that focusing on reconciliation rather than accusation does not result in downplaying the evil of racism. Rather, it suggests that focusing on reconciliation is a more fruitful approach to dealing with the evil that racism creates.

2. This phrase is from the Gettysburg Address given by Abraham Lincoln on November 19, 1863.

12. The Summer of '16

1.   Steve Almasy, "Philando Castile's Sister: He Had a Beautiful Aura," CNN, July 8, 2016, www.cnn.com/2016/07/07/us/philando-castile /index.html.

2.   David DeBolt, "2016 in Review: With Police Shootings, Wheels of Justice Turned Slowly," *The Mercury News* (San Jose, CA), December 26, 2016, www.mercurynews.com/2016/12/26/2016-in-review-with-police -shootings-wheels-ofjustice-turn-slowly/.

13. This Is a Football

1.   Dietrich Bonhoeffer, "The Coming of Jesus in Our Midst," in *A Testament to Freedom: The Essential Writings of Dietrich Bonhoeffer*, rev. ed., eds. Geffrey B. Kelly and Burton Nelson (San Francisco: Harper Collins, 1995), 186.

2.   Love L. Sechrest, "A Former Jew: Paul and the Dialectics of Race" (PhD diss., Duke University, 2006), 179–80.

3.   Sechrest, "Former Jew," 181.

14. Land of Opportunity

1.   "Report of the Special Rapporteur on the Rights of Indigenous People: The Situation of Indigenous Peoples in the United States," United Nations Human Rights Council, United Nations General Assembly, accessed September 4, 2018, www.mitsc.org /documents/104_2012-8-30report-usa-a-hrc-21-47-add1_en.pdf, 5.

2.   Martin Luther King Jr., "'I Have a Dream,' Address Delivered at the March on Washington for Jobs and Freedom," Stanford University, The Martin Luther King Jr. Research and Education Institute, https:// kinginstitute.stanford.edu/king-papers/documents/i-have-dream -address-delivered-march-washington-jobs-and-freedom.

15. It's Tricky

1.   In this chapter, some of the details concerning the churches mentioned have been changed. This reflects the authors' intent to avoid a public critique of any specific congregation. The problems discussed in this chapter plague the entire church in the United States, not just any one congregation, denomination, or nondenominational organization.

2.   Michael Emerson and Christian Smith, *Divided by Faith: Evangelical Religion and the Problem of Race in America* (New York: Oxford University Press, 2000), 139.

3.   Emerson and Smith, *Divided by Faith*, 144.

4.   Emerson and Smith, 145.

5.   Emerson and Smith, 151.

6.   Ronald Heifetz, Alexander Grashow, and Marty Linsky, *The Practice of Adaptive Leadership: Tools and Tactics for Changing Your Organization and the World* (Boston: Harvard Business Press, 2009), 152.

16. Regaining Credibility

1.   Martin Luther King Jr., interview by Ned Brooks et al., *Meet the Press*, NBC, April 17, 1960, http://okra.stanford.edu/transcription /document_images/Vol05Scans/17Apr1960_InterviewonMeetthePress .pdf.

17. Friendship 101

1.   Austin Channing Brown, *I'm Still Here: Black Dignity in a World Made for Whiteness* (New York: Convergent, 2018), 1.

2.   Emily McFarlan Miller, "Austin Channing Brown: White People Are 'Exhausting,'" Religion News Service, May 9, 2018, https://religionnews .com/2018/05/09/white-people-are-exhausting/.

3.   C. S. Lewis, *The Four Loves* (New York: Harcourt Brace Jovanovich, 1960), 96.

4. Cornel West, *Democracy Matters* (New York: Penguin, 2004), 22.

18. Nudging the System

1. Luchina Fisher, "Jessica Chastain Explains Why She Fought for Equal Pay for Octavia Spencer" *ABC News*, June 6, 2018, https://abcnews.go.com/GMA/Culture/jessica-chastain-explains-fought-equal-pay-octavia-spencer/story?id=55691417.

19. How Long?

1. In addition to Scazzero and Peterson's work, the two books mentioned here, we've included an appendix at the end of our book. It contains several resources that deal with spirituality and other subjects that will be helpful to the Christian who desires to join in the battle against racism.

2. Eugene H. Peterson, *Under the Unpredictable Plant: An Exploration in Vocational Holiness* (Grand Rapids, MI: Eerdmans, 1992), 29.

3. Martin Luther King Jr., "'I Have a Dream,' Address Delivered at the March on Washington for Jobs and Freedom," Stanford University, The Martin Luther King Jr. Research and Education Institute, https://kinginstitute.stanford.edu/king-papers/documents/i-have-dream-address-delivered-march-washington-jobs-and-freedom.